Because Flavor is Everything

Recipes with Victoria Taylor's® Seasonings

Victoria Taylor
Founder and President of
Victoria Gourmet, Inc.

Because Flavor is Everything
Recipes with Victoria Taylor's Seasonings

Published by Victoria Gourmet, Inc.
Copyright © 2002 by
Victoria Gourmet, Inc.
Woburn, MA 01801
800-403-8981
www.vgourmet.com

This book is a collection of original recipes.

ISBN: 0-9723215-0-0

Edited, Designed, and Manufactured by

CommunityClassics™
an imprint of
FRP™

P.O. Box 305142
Nashville, Tennessee 37230
800-358-0560

Manufactured in the United States of America

About the Cover

The Cover

All of the recipes for the dishes presented on the front and back covers are included in the chapters of this book.

Front Cover

The centerpiece main dish is Beef Tenderloin prepared with *Victoria Taylor's Peppermill Mix* surrounded by whole garlic heads that have been roasted on *Victoria Taylor's Trapani Sea Salt* and three Veal Birds prepared with *Victoria Taylor's Herbes de Provence*. A close-up of Herbes de Provence is to the left of the tenderloin and a close-up of the Peppermill Mix is below.

The jar on the right side of the cover shows the *Victoria Taylor's Trapani Sea Salt* from Sicily. The colorful tins are presented in several of Victoria's culinary gift collections which feature four tins each of various cooking blends.

Back Cover

The poached pear is prepared with *Victoria Taylor's Mulling Spices* (shown above) and served with a raspberry coulis and garnished with fresh raspberries and sour cream. A close-up of Victoria Taylor's best-selling *Tuscan Seasoning* is below the Tuscan Pasta Salad served with Easy Mediterranean Focaccia topped with shaved Parmigiano-Reggiano and Summer Gazpacho prepared with *Victoria Taylor's New Orleans Seasoning*.

The jars showcase eight of Victoria Taylor's fourteen different cooking blends.

For Jim

Acknowledgments

To my friends and partners I offer my deepest gratitude for their loyalty, hard work, talent, creativity and faith.

Rich Belanger, Carol Coleman, Barbara Gold, Robin Hamilton, Bonnie Henry, Ann Hooper, Deborah Kiernan, Lisa Gouveia, Alex Marren, Kathleen Mirani, Karen and Greg Mitchell, Geoff Raymond and Charlotte Rist.

To my family I offer my love and appreciation for their unwavering support and encouragement.

Jim, Dad, Mom and Harry, Courtney and Joe, Helena, Lela, Anne and Paul, Sterling, Mary and Gordie, Geoff and Kim, Pam and Greg, John, Sue and Lauren.

To all of my investors for their advice, encouragement and support, I offer my sincere thanks. Special thanks to Marshall A. Taylor and KC.

Table of Contents

Foreword

Victoria Gourmet, Inc., was founded in 1998. The company manufactures and sells a line of all-natural seasoning blends for cooking. Victoria Taylor, the company's founder and author of this book, has an extensive background in business and food marketing. She is also an accomplished cook, spending her spare time in the kitchen creating flavors and testing recipes. The combination of her professional experience and her entrepreneurial vision about food and flavor has resulted in a product line with exceptional taste and quality.

Victoria Taylor's Seasonings have been honored with many prestigious awards including the American Tasting Institute's Gold Medal for best tasting gourmet seasoning blends in the country. Victoria's products are sold in gourmet, gift and specialty food stores all over the country. Her website, **www.vgourmet.com**, is a great resource for her customers, offering menus, recipes, cooking tips and gift ideas.

Victoria's customers can purchase her products directly by calling **(866) 972-6879** (8:00 a.m.–5:00 p.m. Pacific time) or by visiting her website. Victoria also has a dedicated toll free number **(800) 403-8981** for her customers to contact her directly for questions, comments and recipe talk.

Victoria Gourmet, Inc. is a member of The National Association of Specialty Food Trade (NASFT), The Massachusetts Specialty Food Association (MSFA), The National Barbecue Association (NBBQA), The International Association of Culinary Professionals (IACP), and The American Institute of Wine & Food (AIWF).

By Bonnie Henry
President & CEO, Hellas International
Board Member, Victoria Gourmet, Inc.

Introduction

I am alone at my desk thinking about cookbook introductions. Looking at my vast cookbook library, I realize that I generally skip the introduction and go right to the recipes.

I love recipes. I love to prepare a new recipe. I love to create recipes, change them, test them and improve them. The creation of my seasoning blends was a nine-month journey paved with hundreds of recipes. Each blend had a mission. The *Toasted Onion Herb Seasoning* had to make the best onion dip and amazing meatloaf. The *Texas Red Seasoning* needed to be perfect in chili recipes and make great fajitas. The *Holiday Seasoning's* mission was to make wonderful stuffing recipes and be the key to a flavorful roasted turkey.

So I blended and tested for nine months. I served chili and stuffing to my husband for dinner for ten straight days. Sometimes the chili was too spicy for him and he couldn't eat it without sweating. Too much ground jalapeño. Then we had 20 different versions of roasted potatoes with *Herbes de Provence*. Next came the meatloaf. I must have put 30 pounds of hamburger down the disposal before I was finally satisfied. I had the best time of my life.

My lifelong passion for food and flavor was the inspiration that led me to create Victoria Taylor's Seasonings. I crave big flavor.

Because Flavor is Everything—Recipes with Victoria Taylor's Seasonings includes over 140 of my tested recipes. My experience in the seasoning world has taught me the importance of recipes. It's the recipes that create confidence and inspire creativity. All of the recipes in this book use seasonings to create wonderfully satisfying flavor. Enjoy these recipes and all the new ones you will be inspired to create.

The Perfect Bite

You know the feeling. Your plate is finally in front of you. Any anxiety you may have felt minutes earlier is gone. For a moment, you admire the food, the colors, textures and the portions. Your salivary glands kick into high gear. You choose a utensil. You arrange your first bite. Perhaps it's a piece of medium-rare sirloin with just a bit of pepper sauce and a piece of sautéed onion. You close your eyes and experience this first perfect bite—the flavors and textures on your tongue—the wonderful aromas. Then comes a deep breath of satisfaction.

You are enjoying one of life's most rewarding pleasures: Flavorful Food.

Victoria

Dips, Breads, Spreads, and Butter

New Orleans Roasted Red Pepper Dip with Victoria Taylor's New Orleans Seasoning

PREPARATION TIME: 10 MINUTES
SERVES: 4

> 1/2 cup roasted red peppers
> 1/2 tablespoon Victoria Taylor's New Orleans Seasoning
> 4 ounces cream cheese, softened

Combine the roasted red peppers, New Orleans Seasoning and cream cheese in a food processor and pulse until well mixed. Serve with crackers, pretzel sticks or crudités for dipping.

Note: This dip has a bright pinkish-red color, so it's great for holidays. Some of my customers swear by it on sandwiches.

Toasted Onion Dip with Victoria Taylor's Toasted Onion Herb Seasoning

PREPARATION TIME: 10 MINUTES
SERVES: 8

> 1 tablespoon Victoria Taylor's Toasted Onion Herb Seasoning
> 1/2 cup sour cream
> 1/2 cup mayonnaise

Combine the sour cream, mayonnaise and Toasted Onion Herb Seasoning in a bowl. Let the dip sit in the refrigerator for 15 to 30 minutes before serving to let the flavors combine. Serve with potato chips or carrots for dipping.

Kalamata Olive Spread with Victoria Taylor's Mediterranean Seasoning

PREPARATION TIME: 10 MINUTES
SERVES: 8

1 cup kalamata olives, pits removed (reserve liquid)
1 tablespoon Victoria Taylor's Mediterranean Seasoning
2 ounces feta cheese
2 ounces cream cheese, softened

Combine the kalamata olives, 1 tablespoon reserved olive liquid, Mediterranean Seasoning, feta cheese and cream cheese in a food processor and pulse until smooth. Serve with crackers or bread. This incredible spread will keep refrigerated for 1 week.

Note: Try to find pitted kalamata olives. If you can't and you don't have an olive pitter (who does?), use the bottom of a coffee cup to split the olives 3 or 4 at a time. Then the pits can be easily removed.

Four-Pepper Goat Cheese Spread with Victoria Taylor's Peppermill Mix

PREPARATION TIME: 5 MINUTES
SERVES: 8 AS AN APPETIZER

  1 to 2 tablespoons Victoria Taylor's Peppermill Mix
  1 small roll goat cheese
  1 tablespoon extra-virgin olive oil

Place the Peppermill Mix in a sealable plastic bag and use a wooden mallet to crush the peppercorns until most of the harder black and white peppercorns have been broken. Peppercorns should still be coarse but not whole. Roll the cheese in the crushed peppercorns and drizzle with the olive oil. Serve with plain crackers.

Note: Freshly crushed peppercorns are very pungent. You may want to reduce the amount of pepper used depending on your taste. I prefer more.

Curry, Cream Cheese and Chutney Spread with Victoria Taylor's Curry

PREPARATION TIME: 15 MINUTES
SERVES: 12

2 tablespoons Victoria Taylor's Curry
1 (9-ounce) jar Major Grey's mango chutney
16 ounces cream cheese, softened
1/2 cup sliced almonds, toasted

Mix the Curry, chutney and cream cheese in a bowl using a wooden spoon. Avoid using a food processor for this spread. The texture should remain chunky and somewhat marbled in appearance. Serve topped with toasted sliced almonds.

Note: My favorite way to present this recipe is by preparing the spread and serving it in a whole pineapple. Slice 1/3 of the pineapple off lengthwise and remove about 1/2 of the pineapple in the remaining larger piece. Fill with the spread and top with the almonds.

Easy Focaccia with Victoria Taylor's Mediterranean Seasoning

PREPARATION TIME: 10 MINUTES / COOKING TIME: 10 MINUTES
SERVES: 4

　1 (16-ounce) package refrigerated bread dough
　1 tablespoon olive oil
　2 tablespoons Victoria Taylor's Mediterranean Seasoning
　2 tablespoons grated Parmesan cheese

Preheat the oven to 500 degrees. Stretch the dough into a 10-inch circle on a pizza pan sprayed with nonstick cooking spray. Brush the dough with the olive oil. Sprinkle with the Mediterranean Seasoning and grated cheese. Bake for 10 minutes or until medium brown.

Note: I love to serve this focaccia with freshly shaved Parmigiano-Reggiano. Use the largest wide opening on your grater to make the shavings.

Easy Classic Pepperoni Pizza with Victoria Taylor's Sicilian Seasoning

<small>Preparation time: 10 minutes / Cooking time: 10 to 12 minutes
Serves: 4 (2 slices each from a 14-inch pizza)</small>

refrigerated pizza dough for one 14-inch pizza
1$\frac{1}{2}$ cups canned crushed tomatoes ($\frac{1}{2}$ of a 28-ounce can)
1 tablespoon Victoria Taylor's Sicilian Seasoning
$\frac{3}{4}$ cup each grated Parmesan cheese and mozzarella cheese
sliced pepperoni

The Crust: For convenience I use the prepared all-purpose dough from the supermarket. It comes in 16-ounce batches, which is perfect for a 14-inch pizza.

The Cooking Surface: There are several options here. The key is to make sure the bottom of the crust gets cooked. A pizza stone or pizza tile works well. I use a greased 14-inch pan with small holes in it. This works well too because the holes help to crisp the dough. Another very effective option for a cooking surface is the top of your broiler pan, which has a pattern of holes or slits in it. Remove the top of your broiler pan and use it as you would a cookie sheet. Whatever cooking surface you choose, spray first with nonstick cooking spray before spreading the dough.

The Pizza: Preheat the oven to 550 degrees. Shape the pizza dough on your work surface or on the pan with your hands by pulling and stretching it. Combine the crushed tomatoes and Sicilian Seasoning in a bowl and mix well. Spread the sauce evenly over the dough. Sprinkle with the grated cheeses. Top with pepperoni. Bake for 10 to 12 minutes. Let stand for 5 minutes before slicing.

Note: If you really are going to live with just 2 slices of pizza per person, then a salad would help to round out the meal. Spicy food lovers can sprinkle extra Sicilian Seasoning on their slices as needed.

Hot Tuscan Bread with Victoria Taylor's Tuscan Seasoning

PREPARATION TIME: 15 MINUTES / COOKING TIME: 15 MINUTES
SERVES: 6

1 (16-ounce) package refrigerated bread dough or pizza dough
2 tablespoons olive oil
2 tablespoons Victoria Taylor's Tuscan Seasoning

Let the dough rest at room temperature for 10 to 15 minutes before you begin. Preheat the oven to 475 degrees. Shape the dough into a 6×12-inch rectangle. Brush with the olive oil. Sprinkle with the Tuscan Seasoning. Roll the dough jelly roll fashion to make a 12-inch long loaf. Place on a baking sheet. Bake for 15 minutes or until medium brown.

Note: I always keep a couple of packages of bread dough or pizza dough in the freezer to make bread or focaccia when I'm in the mood and don't want to make a trip to the store just for bread.

Tuscan Bread Dipping Oil with Victoria Taylor's Tuscan Seasoning

PREPARATION TIME: 5 MINUTES
SERVES: 4

1/2 cup extra-virgin olive oil
1 tablespoon Victoria Taylor's Tuscan Seasoning
1 1/2 teaspoons white wine vinegar

Combine the olive oil, Tuscan Seasoning and vinegar in a bowl and mix well. Serve with sliced French or Italian bread.

16

This recipe may also be made very successfully with my Herbes de Provence, Sicilian Seasoning or Mediterranean Seasoning.

Note: The quality of the olive oil is very important for this recipe. Choose your favorite extra-virgin olive oil whenever you make bread dipping oil.

Tuscan Garlic Butter with Victoria Taylor's Tuscan Seasoning

PREPARATION TIME: 10 MINUTES
SERVES: 8

1/2 cup (1 stick) butter, softened
6 cloves garlic, minced
2 tablespoons Victoria Taylor's Tuscan Seasoning

Place softened butter in a bowl. Add the garlic and Tuscan Seasoning and mix well. Spoon butter mixture onto the center of an 8-inch piece of plastic wrap. Shape into an 1 1/2-inch-diameter tube, twisting both ends of the plastic wrap to seal. Chill until ready to serve. Cut 1/2-inch slices to use on bread, grilled chicken or mashed potatoes.

Note: I love butter. I never use a butter substitute. The flavor of butter in cooking simply cannot be matched.

Spicy Cheddar-Chive Rounds with Victoria Taylor's New Orleans Seasoning

PREPARATION TIME: 20 MINUTES
REFRIGERATION TIME: 1 TO 2 HOURS / COOKING TIME: 30 MINUTES
MAKES: 100 CRACKERS

    3 cups grated sharp Cheddar cheese
    1 cup freshly grated Parmesan cheese
    3 tablespoons dried chives
    2 tablespoons Victoria Taylor's New Orleans Seasoning
    1½ cups all-purpose flour
    6 tablespoons cold unsalted butter, cut into pieces
    ½ teaspoon salt
    ¾ cup buttermilk

Combine the grated cheeses, chives and New Orleans Seasoning in a large bowl and toss to mix. Combine the flour, butter and salt in a food processor. Pulse until the mixture resembles cornmeal. Add the flour to the cheese mixture and toss until well mixed. Stir in the buttermilk using a fork. Mix just until the dough can be gathered into a ball. Turn the dough onto a lightly floured surface and knead it for 10 to 15 seconds. Divide the dough in half and roll each piece into a log 1 inch in diameter. Wrap the dough logs in waxed paper and refrigerate until firm, about 1 to 2 hours (the dough may be frozen for up to 2 months). Preheat the oven to 325 degrees. Cut the logs into ⅛-inch-thick slices and arrange the slices about ½ inch apart on 2 large baking sheets. Bake for 15 minutes. Switch the sheets and bake the crackers for 15 minutes longer or until golden brown. Crackers may be stored up to 10 days in a tightly sealed storage container.

Note: These crackers are absolutely addictive. They are crunchy (but not too crunchy) and spicy and delicious.

Appetizers and Hors d'Oeuvres

Tomato Crostini with Mediterranean Herbs and Olives with Victoria Taylor's Mediterranean Seasoning

PREPARATION TIME: 20 MINUTES / COOKING TIME: 1 HOUR
SERVES: 6 (4 CROSTINI EACH)

12 medium plum tomatoes, halved lengthwise
1/4 cup extra-virgin olive oil
3 tablespoons Victoria Taylor's Mediterranean Seasoning, divided
24 (1/4-inch) slices French baguette
2 cups kalamata olives, pits removed (reserve liquid)
4 ounces feta cheese
4 ounces cream cheese, softened
chopped fresh oregano (optional for garnish)

Preheat the oven to 350 degrees. Place tomato halves cut sides up in a baking dish just large enough to hold them. Drizzle with 1/4 cup olive oil and sprinkle with 1 tablespoon of the Mediterranean Seasoning. Roast for 1 hour or until tomatoes are tender and wrinkled. Brush bread slices with additional olive oil. Place on a baking sheet. Bake until lightly toasted, about 15 to 20 minutes. Combine olives, 2 tablespoons reserved olive liquid, remaining 2 tablespoons Mediterranean Seasoning, feta cheese and cream cheese in a food processor. Pulse until smooth. Brush each piece of toast with 1 teaspoon olive mixture and top with a roasted tomato. Garnish with a sprinkle of oregano. Reheat in oven if needed.

Olive and Roasted Pepper Crostini with Victoria Taylor's Mediterranean Seasoning

PREPARATION TIME: 30 MINUTES / COOKING TIME: 1 MINUTE
SERVES: 4 TO 6

1 red bell pepper, halved and seeded
1 yellow bell pepper, halved and seeded
1 loaf French bread
3/4 cup pitted black kalamata olives
1 tablespoon capers
2 teaspoons Victoria Taylor's Mediterranean Seasoning
3 tablespoons extra-virgin olive oil
1 tablespoon chopped flat-leaf Italian parsley (optional)
4 balls of fresh mozzarella cheese (about 10 ounces)

Preheat the broiler. Canned roasted peppers may be used, but I prefer to make them fresh. Press the bell pepper halves flat with your hand and broil them skin side up until the skins are charred black, about 10 minutes. Remove the peppers from the broiler and place them in a sealable plastic bag for 20 minutes. Slice the bread into twenty 1/4-inch slices and toast the bread in the broiler until light brown, about 30 to 40 seconds per side. Set the toasted bread aside. Now remove the peppers from the plastic bag, peel off the charred skins, slice them into 1/4-inch strips and set aside. Combine the olives, capers, Mediterranean Seasoning and olive oil in a food processor and pulse until smooth. Stir the chopped parsley into the mixture. Slice the cheese into about twenty 1/8- to 1/4-inch slices. Spread a thin layer of the olive mixture on each piece of toast, top with a slice of cheese, a strip of red pepper and a strip of yellow pepper. Broil the crostini until the cheese begins to melt, about 30 seconds. Serve immediately.

Note: Canned or jarred roasted red peppers may be used for this recipe. It's just hard to find yellow ones and the color is so appealing on the finished crostini.

Spanish-Style Stuffed Red Peppers with Victoria Taylor's Mediterranean Seasoning

PREPARATION TIME: 10 MINUTES / COOKING TIME: 10 MINUTES
SERVES: 4 AS AN APPETIZER

    8 Spanish piquillo peppers, canned or jarred (reserve liquid)
    4 ounces cream cheese or goat cheese
    2 tablespoons fresh lemon juice
    1 tablespoon Victoria Taylor's Mediterranean Seasoning
    salt and pepper to taste
    2 or 3 strips proscuitto or smoked ham, finely diced
    extra-virgin olive oil (optional for garnish)
    3 tablespoons toasted pine nuts (optional for garnish)

Preheat the oven to 325 degrees. Remove seeds from peppers if necessary. Combine the cream cheese, lemon juice, Mediterranean Seasoning, 1 teaspoon reserved pepper liquid, salt, pepper and prosciutto in a bowl and mix well. Stuff peppers with equal portions of the mixture, about 1 tablespoon per pepper and place on a baking sheet. Bake for about 10 minutes. Arrange on a platter and garnish with a drizzle of olive oil and a scattering of toasted pine nuts. Salt cod or other cooked fish may be substituted for the proscuitto. Serve with a delicate white wine, such as a Spanish albarino or a pinot grigio. This is a great appetizer before a seafood entrée. It's also nice served on a bed of seasonal greens.

Note: I'm a huge fan of prosciutto. It's got a flavor that is salty, unique, and very satisfactory. If you can, find a butcher who sells the real thing and he will cut it paper thin for you. Use any extra for cantaloupe wrapped in prosciutto.

Classic Moroccan Hummus with Victoria Taylor's Moroccan Seasoning

PREPARATION TIME: 10 MINUTES
SERVES: 6 TO 8

1 (19-ounce) can chick-peas, drained
2 to 3 tablespoons Victoria Taylor's Moroccan Seasoning (add more to taste)
1/2 teaspoon salt
2 tablespoons fresh lemon juice
6 tablespoons extra-virgin olive oil
finely chopped red onion (optional for garnish)
lemon (optional for garnish)

To Prepare: Place the chick-peas, Moroccan Seasoning, salt, lemon juice and olive oil in a food processor. Pulse until the mixture is smooth and creamy.

To Serve: To show off the rich color of this hummus, choose a serving bowl with a contrasting color such as blue, green or white. Serve with a basket of pita triangles or small crackers such as mini stoned wheat crackers. Garnish with red onion and a squeeze of lemon.

Note: To keep the hummus cool, fill a small sealable plastic bag with ice. Place the bag in a second bag to protect from leakage. Place the plastic bag of ice on a plate and cover with a cloth napkin. Now nestle the bowl of hummus on the napkin. The ice will keep the hummus cool for up to 4 hours.

Spinach-Stuffed Portobello Mushrooms with Victoria Taylor's Sicilian Seasoning

PREPARATION TIME: 20 MINUTES / COOKING TIME: 25 MINUTES
SERVES: 8 TO 10

    30 baby portobellos (2$1/2$ to 2$3/4$ inches in diameter)
    2 tablespoons butter
    1$1/2$ cups chopped onions
    $1/2$ teaspoon salt
    4 teaspoons Victoria Taylor's Sicilian Seasoning
    1 (10-ounce) package frozen chopped spinach, thawed and
        squeezed dry
    $1/2$ cup soft white bread crumbs
    1$1/2$ cups grated Parmesan cheese
    $3/4$ cup whipping cream
    3 eggs

Use a spoon to scoop out the mushroom stems and gills, leaving the mushroom intact. Chop the stems and gills finely. Melt the butter in a medium saucepan. Add the onions, salt and Sicilian Seasoning. Sauté for 5 minutes and remove from heat. Preheat the oven to 375 degrees. Combine the onion mixture, spinach, chopped mushroom stems and gills, bread crumbs, grated cheese, cream and eggs in a medium bowl and mix well. Spoon the stuffing into the mushrooms and arrange on a baking sheet. Bake for 25 minutes. Serve immediately.

Note: What a great hors d'oeuvre. You can prepare the mushrooms up to 30 minutes before cooking, then bake as directed.

Roasted Potato Caviar Bites with Sour Cream and Radish Garnish with Victoria Taylor's Herbes de Provence

PREPARATION TIME: 20 MINUTES / COOKING TIME: 30 MINUTES
SERVES: 4 (ABOUT 4 BITES EACH)

4 (1- to 2-inch wide) red bliss potatoes
4 teaspoons Victoria Taylor's Herbes de Provence
2 tablespoons olive oil
1/2 cup sour cream
1 small jar red caviar
radishes, halved and sliced (optional for garnish)

Preheat the oven to 375 degrees. Cut the potatoes into 1/4-inch slices, discarding the small ends. You should end up with 3 to 5 slices per potato. Toss potato slices with the Herbes de Provence and olive oil in a sealable plastic bag. Arrange potatoes in a single layer on a baking sheet and roast for 30 minutes, turning once. Remove potatoes and cool just until warm. Top each with a spoonful of sour cream and a pinch of red caviar. Garnish with an individual slice of radish and serve.

Stuffed Red Potato Bites with Victoria Taylor's Tuscan Seasoning

PREPARATION TIME: 30 MINUTES / COOKING TIME: 45 MINUTES
SERVES: 8 AS APPETIZER

    11 small red bliss or new red potatoes, divided
    1 tablespoon olive oil
    1/2 teaspoon salt
    1 large carrot, peeled and cut into 1-inch pieces
    1 small white onion, peeled and left whole
    2 tablespoons milk
    1 tablespoon butter
    1 tablespoon Victoria Taylor's Tuscan Seasoning
    3 slices bacon, cooked (optional)

Preheat the oven to 350 degrees. Cut 8 of the red potatoes in half. Trim the bottom off of the potato halves so the halves stand flat. Scoop a hole in the center of each half and discard the scooped out portion. The red potato "cups" should be about 1/4 inch thick. Now toss the potato "cups" gently with the olive oil and salt. Arrange on a baking sheet. Roast for 30 minutes or until tender. Remove from oven and let cool. To prepare the stuffing, boil the remaining 3 unpeeled red potatoes, carrot and onion in water to cover in a small saucepan until tender, about 15 minutes; drain. Combine the cooked vegetables, milk, butter, Tuscan Seasoning and cooked bacon in a food processor. Process until almost smooth. To assemble the potatoes, use a small spoon to fill the red potatoes with the stuffing mixture. Arrange the stuffed potatoes on a platter and serve.

Note: These can be prepared several hours ahead. Just reheat them in a 350-degree oven for 5 to 10 minutes before serving.

Soups, Salads, and Sandwiches

Spicy Butternut Squash and Apple Soup with Victoria Taylor's New Orleans Seasoning

PREPARATION TIME: 45 MINUTES / COOKING TIME: 10 MINUTES
SERVES: 6 AS A MAIN COURSE, OR 8 AS A FIRST COURSE

2 large butternut squash, peeled and cut into 2-inch pieces
2 tablespoons butter
2 tablespoons olive oil
3 carrots, grated
2 medium onions, chopped
2 tablespoons Victoria Taylor's New Orleans Seasoning
1 teaspoon salt
1/2 cup pine nuts, divided
3 MacIntosh apples, peeled and cut into 1-inch pieces
3 cans chicken broth
2 tablespoons Calvados (apple brandy)
1/2 cup dry white wine
sour cream (optional for garnish)

Place the squash in a large saucepan with enough water to cover and bring to a low boil. Cook until tender, about 15 minutes. Drain and place in a large bowl. Heat the butter and olive oil in a large skillet until hot but not smoking. Add the carrots, onions, New Orleans Seasoning, salt and 1/4 cup of the pine nuts. Sauté for 5 minutes over medium heat. Add the apples and sauté for another 3 minutes. Now add 1 can of the chicken broth and the Calvados. Bring back to a boil and boil for about 2 minutes longer. Remove from heat. Add the apple mixture to the squash. Transfer the mixture in batches to a blender or a food processor to purée. Place the thick purée in a large saucepan. Now add the remaining 2 cans chicken broth and the white wine. Bring the soup back to a low simmer. Simmer for 10 minutes before serving. While the soup is reheating, brown the remaining 1/4 cup pine nuts in an ungreased skillet over high heat for 2 to 3 minutes, stirring constantly.

Garnish the soup with a spoonful of sour cream and the toasted pine nuts.

Note: This soup makes a wonderful first course for entertaining. It's spicy but not too spicy. An alternative garnish that is also delicious for this soup is Homemade Croutons (below).

Homemade Croutons

PREPARATION TIME: 10 MINUTES / COOKING TIME: 10 MINUTES
MAKES: 2 CUPS

- 3 tablespoons butter
- 3 tablespoons olive oil
- 3 cloves garlic, minced
- 2 cups cubed Italian or French bread
- 1 tablespoon chopped chives
- 2/3 cup finely grated Parmesan cheese

Heat the butter and olive oil in a large skillet until hot but not smoking. Stir in the garlic. Add the bread. Cook until browned on all sides, stirring frequently. Remove to a bowl. Add the chives and Parmesan cheese and toss to coat.

Summer Gazpacho with Victoria Taylor's New Orleans Seasoning

PREPARATION TIME: 45 MINUTES
SERVES: 6

2 large tomatoes, unpeeled and seeded
1 large cucumber, peeled and seeded
1 green bell pepper, cored and seeded
1 red bell pepper, cored and seeded
1 medium red onion
32 ounces tomato juice
2 tablespoons Victoria Taylor's New Orleans Seasoning
1 tablespoon sugar
1/2 cup extra-virgin olive oil
1/3 cup red wine vinegar
salt to taste
sour cream (optional for garnish)

Chop the tomatoes, cucumber, bell peppers and onion in a food processor fairly finely. Combine the tomato mixture and tomato juice in a large bowl and mix well. Now add the New Orleans Seasoning, sugar, olive oil and vinegar and mix well. Stir in salt. Chill the gazpacho before serving and garnish each serving with a spoonful of sour cream.

All-Purpose Homemade Chicken Stock with Victoria Taylor's Herbes de Provence

PREPARATION TIME: 15 MINUTES / COOKING TIME: 3 HOURS
MAKES: 3½ QUARTS STOCK

5 pounds chicken pieces (light and dark meat)
8 whole cloves
2 medium white onions, unpeeled and quartered
leafy tops (top ⅓) of a bunch of celery
4 large sprigs of fresh Italian parsley
1 leek, cleaned and cut into 3-inch pieces
2 large carrots, scrubbed and cut into 3-inch pieces
4 cloves garlic, unpeeled
2 teaspoons salt
4 teaspoons Victoria Taylor's Herbes de Provence
1 gallon water (spring water preferred)
2 tablespoons cider vinegar

Rinse the chicken, leaving the skin on. Use a very large soup pot to cook this stock. Place the chicken in the pot. Push the cloves into the skins of each of the onion quarters and add them to the pot. Add celery, parsley, leek, carrots, garlic, salt and Herbes de Provence. Now add the water and vinegar to the pot. Simmer for 3 hours, adding water as needed. If you are looking for a very concentrated stock, add less water. Water may always be added later when you are using the stock. Remove the stock from the heat and strain it into a large bowl. Cool for at least 20 minutes but not more than 40 minutes before transferring to storage in the refrigerator or freezer. Discard all the solids; the chicken will be tasteless after the long cooking time. When you are ready to use the stock, remove the fat that has formed on the surface and discard it.

Note: This is my basic chicken stock for soups and sauces. The flavor of homemade stock is far better than canned. You may also freeze the stock for up to 3 months.

Spicy Corn Salad with Victoria Taylor's New Orleans Seasoning

PREPARATION TIME: 20 MINUTES / COOKING TIME: 20 MINUTES
SERVES: 8

1 teaspoon salt
10 ears of corn, husks removed
2 tablespoons olive oil
1 large yellow onion, finely chopped
3 cloves fresh garlic, minced
1 tablespoon Victoria Taylor's New Orleans Seasoning
1 small jalapeño pepper, finely chopped
1 large red, orange or yellow bell pepper, cut into 1/2-inch pieces
1 large red or orange tomato, finely chopped

Bring a large pot of water to a rolling boil. Add the salt and corn. Return water to a boil and cook corn for 8 minutes. Rinse the cooked corn in cold water to cool and slice the corn from the cobs. Heat the olive oil in a large skillet and add the onion and garlic. Sauté in the hot oil for 5 minutes. Mix in the New Orleans Seasoning and add the jalapeño, bell pepper and corn. Sauté for 3 minutes. Add the tomato and sauté for another minute. Refrigerate before serving.

Note: This salad keeps well in the refrigerator for up to 3 days. When corn is in season, don't miss the chance to try this recipe.

Sicilian Tomato, Cucumber and Feta Salad with Victoria Taylor's Sicilian Seasoning

PREPARATION TIME: 30 MINUTES
SERVES: 4

4 medium tomatoes, cut into $1/2$-inch pieces
1 large cucumber, peeled, seeded and cut into $1/2$-inch slices
1 medium white onion, cut into $1/2$-inch pieces
1 large green bell pepper, cut into 1-inch pieces
$2/3$ cup crumbled feta cheese
3 tablespoons extra-virgin olive oil
1 tablespoon red wine vinegar
2 tablespoons Victoria Taylor's Sicilian Seasoning

Combine the tomatoes, cucumber, onion, green pepper, crumbled cheese, olive oil, vinegar and Sicilian Seasoning in a bowl and stir gently. Let salad stand for 15 minutes or more before serving.

Note: I often use a full cup (or more) of feta cheese in the salad. Served with French or Italian bread, this Greek-style salad makes a satisfying light meal.

Tuscan Pasta Salad with Victoria Taylor's Tuscan Seasoning

PREPARATION TIME: 10 MINUTES / COOKING TIME: 10 MINUTES
SERVES: 4

1 pound spiral pasta
2 cups baby carrots, sliced
1 red bell pepper, cut into $1/4$-inch pieces
1 yellow bell pepper, cut into $1/4$-inch pieces
1 cup asiago cheese, grated
$1/4$ cup olive oil
1 tablespoon apple cider vinegar
3 tablespoons Victoria Taylor's Tuscan Seasoning

Cook the pasta using the package directions; drain and cool. Mix carrots, bell peppers, grated cheese, olive oil, vinegar and Tuscan Seasoning in a large bowl and mix well. Add the pasta and toss to mix; serve.

Note: This salad has amazing flavor and color. It keeps well in sealable plastic bags for up to 5 days.

The Best Curried Chicken Salad with Victoria Taylor's Curry

PREPARATION TIME: 15 MINUTES / COOKING TIME: 15 MINUTES
REFRIGERATION TIME: 1 HOUR
SERVES: 8

6 boneless skinless chicken breast halves (about 2 to 2½ pounds)
4 teaspoons Victoria Taylor's Curry
½ teaspoon salt
1 cup mayonnaise
¼ cup currants or raisins
¼ cup peanuts
1 bunch scallions, finely sliced (pale green and white portions only)

Place enough water to cover the chicken in a medium saucepan. Bring to a boil. Add the chicken. Return to a boil and reduce heat. Simmer just until cooked, about 15 minutes. Place the cooked chicken breasts on a plate in a single layer, cover with plastic wrap and refrigerate until cooled, about 1 hour. While chicken is cooking, combine the Curry, salt, mayonnaise, currants, peanuts and scallions in a medium bowl and mix well. Cover and refrigerate. When the chicken is cool, cut into ¼-inch pieces and combine with the Curry mixture. Serve immediately or after additional refrigeration.

Note: For Curried Chicken Sandwiches, spread some Major Grey's Mango Chutney on bread and top with the chicken salad and lettuce, if desired.

Chicken Salad with Blue Cheese and Roasted Walnuts with Victoria Taylor's Holiday Seasoning

PREPARATION TIME: 15 MINUTES / COOKING TIME: 30 MINUTES
SERVES: 4

4 boneless skinless chicken breasts
1/4 cup white bread crumbs
4 teaspoons Victoria Taylor's Holiday Seasoning
4 tablespoons butter
1/2 cup chopped walnuts
3/4 cup crumbled blue cheese
3/4 cup raisins
1 cup mayonnaise

Preheat the oven to 350 degrees. Pound the chicken breasts to an even 1/2-inch thickness. Sprinkle each chicken breast with 1 tablespoon bread crumbs and 1 teaspoon Holiday Seasoning. Dot each on top and bottom with 1 tablespoon butter. Arrange the chicken in a baking dish. Bake for 30 minutes. After the chicken cools enough to handle, cut the chicken breasts into 1/2-inch pieces. Toast the walnuts in a sauté pan over medium heat for about 5 minutes. Combine the crumbled cheese, toasted walnuts, raisins and mayonnaise in a large bowl and mix well. Add the chicken and mix well. Serve warm or refrigerate first and serve cold.

Note: My favorite way to serve this salad is with endive leaves. Fill each endive leaf with chicken salad and eat with your hands.

Layered Nacho Salad with Victoria Taylor's Texas Red Seasoning

PREPARATION TIME: 20 MINUTES / REFRIGERATION TIME: 30 TO 60 MINUTES
SERVES: 4

2 large avocados, peeled and pits removed
2 tomatoes, cut into 1/4-inch pieces
2 tablespoons Victoria Taylor's Texas Red Seasoning
2 heads romaine lettuce (crisp end only), coarsely chopped
3 cups shredded cooked chicken
3 cups broken tortilla chips
1 can black beans, drained and rinsed
6 scallions, chopped
1 orange or red bell pepper, cut into 1/4-inch pieces
1 cup grated Cheddar cheese
salt and pepper to taste

Combine the avocados, tomatoes and Texas Red Seasoning in a bowl. Mash together to make guacamole. Layer the lettuce, chicken, chips, beans, scallions, bell pepper and grated cheese in a clear glass bowl to see the colorful layers. Top with the guacamole. Cover and chill for 30 to 60 minutes before serving. Season with salt and pepper to taste. Serve with additional grated cheese, salsa and tortilla chips.

Note: This is a great summer dish, especially when you have all the ripe tomatoes to use up. Ground beef may be substituted for the chicken.

Quick Creamy Garlic and Herb Dressing with Victoria Taylor's Mediterranean Seasoning

PREPARATION TIME: 10 MINUTES
MAKES: 1 CUP DRESSING

2 tablespoons red wine vinegar
1 tablespoon Victoria Taylor's Mediterranean Seasoning
1 pasteurized egg
3/4 cup extra-virgin olive oil
ground black pepper to taste

Combine the vinegar and Mediterranean Seasoning in a small bowl. Place the egg in a food processor and pulse until smooth. Add the vinegar mixture to the egg and process to mix well. Keep the food processor on and gradually pour the olive oil into the dressing. Add pepper to taste. The dressing will keep refrigerated for up to 3 days.

Note: Use this dressing for tossed green salads and spinach salad. It's also great with artichokes. Use the dressing in place of butter for dipping the cooked artichoke leaves.

Roasted Red Pepper, Salami and Artichoke Roll-Up with Victoria Taylor's Tuscan Seasoning

PREPARATION TIME: 10 MINUTES
SERVES: 4

1 (6-ounce) jar artichoke hearts, drained
2 tablespoons Victoria Taylor's Tuscan Seasoning
1/4 pound sliced salami
1/2 pound sliced provolone cheese
1/2 cup roasted red peppers
4 pieces large flatbread (plain or sun-dried tomato flavor)
2 cups coarsely chopped greens (spring mix or watercress)

Crush the artichoke hearts with the Tuscan Seasoning in a bowl using a fork until well mixed. Layer the salami, sliced cheese, red peppers and artichoke mixture along the center of the flatbread. Top with the mixed greens. Roll up to enclose filling and secure with a wooden pick. Serve chilled or heated. To heat, make roll-up without the lettuce, heat in a 325-degree oven for 15 to 20 minutes. Then add the lettuce and serve.

Note: This great recipe comes from my friend Nancy Hurley. Nancy is one of my first and most loyal customers. She sells my seasonings at her store, The Roasted Pepper, in Charleston, West Virginia, where she also serves her customers many delicious recipes she prepares using her favorite Victoria Taylor's Seasonings. I'm sure you will agree, her roll-up recipe is great.

Moroccan-Style Grilled Cheddar Cheese Sandwiches with Victoria Taylor's Moroccan Seasoning

PREPARATION TIME: 10 MINUTES / COOKING TIME: 8 MINUTES
SERVES: 4

$1/4$ cup Dijon mustard
$1/4$ cup mayonnaise
1 beef steak tomato, seeds removed and cut into $1/4$-inch pieces
2 tablespoons Victoria Taylor's Moroccan Seasoning
$1/2$ pound cheese (Cheddar, Gouda or American), thinly sliced
8 ($1/2$-inch-thick) sourdough bread slices
4 tablespoons butter, melted

Mix the mustard, mayonnaise, tomato and Moroccan Seasoning in a bowl. Spread between slices of cheese. Place cheese between slices of bread. Brush the outside of both sides of the sandwich with the melted butter. Heat a large nonstick pan over medium heat. Add sandwiches to the pan and cook until bread is browned, about 3 minutes. Turn sandwiches to other side, then cover the pan. Continue to grill until cheese melts, about 3 to 5 minutes.

Note: This sandwich is full of flavor. Savor every bite. Serve with chips and pickles.

Sides

Mediterranean Stuffed Artichokes with Victoria Taylor's Mediterranean Seasoning

PREPARATION TIME: 1 HOUR / COOKING TIME: 1 HOUR
SERVES: 6 OR 8

1 small loaf French or Italian bread
   (enough for 2^1/$_2$ cups of bread crumbs)
^{3}/$_4$ cup grated Parmesan cheese
2 tablespoons Victoria Taylor's Mediterranean Seasoning
^{1}/$_2$ cup extra-virgin olive oil
6 large or 8 small artichokes
1^1/$_2$ cups dry white wine or white vermouth

Making the Stuffing: Preheat the oven to 400 degrees. Slice the bread and toast it on a baking sheet in the oven until dry but not brown, about 10 minutes. Cool. Place the bread in a food processor and pulse into coarse crumbs. You should have about 2^1/$_2$ cups. Mix the bread crumbs, grated cheese and Mediterranean Seasoning in a bowl. Add the olive oil to the stuffing and mix well.

Preparing the Chokes for Stuffing: Slice the stems off at the base of the choke and cut the top third of the choke off. Trim the points off all the leaves with a pair of kitchen scissors. Start to open the choke with your hands and scrape out the hairy choke center with a spoon. Be aggressive. This is the fun part. Stuff each choke with prepared stuffing, pushing the stuffing in the center and between the larger outer leaves.

Cooking the Chokes: Use a casserole or pan just large enough to hold the chokes. The chokes can stand slightly higher than the edge of the pan if needed. Drizzle the wine over the chokes. Add water to the pan until the chokes are sitting in 1$^{1}/_{2}$ inches of liquid. Bring to a boil and cover loosely with foil. Reduce the heat. Simmer until tender, about 1 hour. Add more water or wine to the cooking liquid as needed. Remove chokes from pan with a large pair of tongs.

Note: This one might sound a little daunting, but it's worth it. If they are presented as a first course, I serve them on a large plate so there is plenty of room for discarded leaves. If they are with a main course, you will need to add a few bowls to the table for leaf disposal.

Steamed Asparagus and Garlic Herb Cream with Victoria Taylor's Mediterranean Seasoning

PREPARATION TIME: 15 MINUTES / COOKING TIME: 5 MINUTES
SERVES: 4

- 2 pounds fresh asparagus
- 3 tablespoons fresh lime juice
- 1 tablespoon Victoria Taylor's Mediterranean Seasoning
- 1 pasteurized egg
- 2 cloves fresh garlic
- 3/4 cup extra-virgin olive oil
- pepper to taste

Trim the asparagus and steam until crisp-tender, about 5 minutes. Rinse with cold water to stop the cooking process and retain the bright green color. Combine the lime juice and Mediterranean Seasoning in a small bowl and mix well. Place the egg and garlic in a food processor and pulse until smooth. Add the lime mixture and while the food processor is on, gradually pour in the olive oil. Add pepper to taste and serve over the asparagus. The asparagus may be served chilled or warmed. If the dressing is made ahead (up to 2 days), bring it to room temperature before serving.

El Paso Rice and Beans with Victoria Taylor's Texas Red Seasoning

PREPARATION TIME: 25 MINUTES / COOKING TIME: 35 MINUTES
SERVES: 6

1 pound ground beef
1 green bell pepper, chopped (1-inch pieces)
1 yellow onion, chopped
1 (28-ounce) can crushed tomatoes
2 tablespoons Victoria Taylor's Texas Red Seasoning
1 cup white rice
1 (19-ounce) can red kidney beans
4 ounces Monterey Jack or Cheddar cheese, shredded

Brown the ground beef in a large skillet; drain. Remove from skillet. Add green pepper and onion to skillet and sauté until tender, about 6 to 8 minutes. Add ground beef to onion and pepper in skillet, then add the tomatoes, Texas Red Seasoning and rice. Bring to a boil. Then reduce heat and simmer for 15 minutes, stirring occasionally. Preheat the oven to 350 degrees. Transfer ground beef mixture to a large covered casserole. Add beans and mix well. Bake for 25 minutes. Remove from oven and sprinkle shredded cheese on top. Return to oven. Bake, uncovered, for 8 to 10 minutes or until cheese is melted.

Note: Use any kind of canned beans, such as pinto beans, garbanzo beans, or black beans, for this easy recipe.

Curried Green Beans with Bacon and Pine Nuts with Victoria Taylor's Curry

Preparation time: 35 minutes / Cooking time: 10 minutes
Serves: 4

1 teaspoon sea salt
1 pound fresh green beans
4 slices bacon
1 medium onion, chopped
1/2 cup pine nuts
1 tablespoon Victoria Taylor's Curry
1 (14-ounce) can diced tomatoes, undrained
salt and pepper to taste

Bring a medium saucepan of water with 1 teaspoon sea salt to a rapid boil. Add the green beans and cook for 5 minutes. Drain and rinse in cold water to stop them from cooking and set aside. Cut the bacon into 1/2-inch pieces and cook over medium heat in a large skillet. Drain, reserving 1 tablespoon of bacon dripping, and set aside. Using the bacon drippings, cook the onion, pine nuts and Curry for 5 minutes, stirring frequently. Add the tomatoes and cook until the sauce begins to boil. Add the green beans and cook for 5 minutes or until heated through. Add the crumbled bacon. Cook for 1 minute longer, stirring constantly. Season with salt and pepper to taste and serve.

Note: For bright green, al dente vegetables, add them to boiling water seasoned with sea salt and cook for 5 minutes. Remove from heat and rinse with cold water immediately to stop the cooking process. Sauté briefly to reheat.

Curried Carrot and Raisin Pilaf with Cashews with Victoria Taylor's Curry

PREPARATION TIME: 20 MINUTES / COOKING TIME: 20 MINUTES
SERVES: 4

2 cups basmati rice
3 tablespoons butter
1 large onion, chopped
3 tablespoons Victoria Taylor's Curry
1/2 cup golden raisins
2 large carrots, cut into 1/4- to 1/2-inch pieces
3 cups water
1 teaspoon sea salt
1/2 cup salted cashew halves

Rinse the rice in cold water and set aside. In a medium saucepan with a lid, heat the butter until hot but not brown. Add the onion and sauté for 2 minutes. Stir in the Curry until well blended. Add the rice, raisins and carrots to the pan. Cook until the rice is well colored, about 2 minutes, stirring constantly. Add the water and sea salt to the pan and stir well. Bring the pilaf to a boil and then reduce the heat. Cover the pan and simmer for 20 minutes. Remove from heat. Stir in the cashews and let stand, covered, for 10 minutes before serving.

Note: Basmati rice is now available in most grocery stores. It has a completely different taste and texture than plain rice. It is a key flavor component in this recipe.

Cajun Corn Bread Casserole with Victoria Taylor's New Orleans Seasoning

PREPARATION TIME: 25 MINUTES / COOKING TIME: 50 MINUTES
SERVES: 8

Bottom Layer
1 (15-ounce) can regular whole kernel corn, drained
4 ounces grated sharp Cheddar cheese
1 tablespoon Victoria Taylor's New Orleans Seasoning
1/2 cup sour cream

Top Layer
1 (8 1/2-ounce) package corn bread mix
2 large eggs
1/2 cup milk
1 (4-ounce) can chopped green chiles, drained
1 (15-ounce) can creamed corn
1/2 cup chopped onion
4 ounces grated sharp Cheddar cheese
1 teaspoon Victoria Taylor's New Orleans Seasoning

Preheat the oven to 425 degrees. Use a high-sided round casserole 8 to 9 inches in diameter or use a high-sided 8- or 9-inch square pan.

For the Bottom Layer: Mix the corn, grated cheese, New Orleans Seasoning and sour cream in a bowl and spread on the bottom of the casserole.

For the Top Layer: Mix the corn bread mix, eggs, milk, green chiles, corn, onion, grated cheese and New Orleans Seasoning in a bowl and pour the mixture on top of the bottom layer. Bake, uncovered, for 50 minutes or until the top is golden brown.

Note: This is a four-star family favorite. I can't count the number of times I have heard, "Vic, will you please make that corn bread thing? Please?"

Firecracker Corn Cobs with Victoria Taylor's Texas Red Seasoning

PREPARATION TIME: 10 MINUTES / COOKING TIME: 15 TO 20 MINUTES
SERVES: 4

2 teaspoons butter, softened
2 teaspoons Victoria Taylor's Texas Red Seasoning
4 ears of fresh corn

Prepare the grill for cooking. Combine the butter and Texas Red Seasoning in a bowl and mix well. Coat each ear of corn with the butter mixture. Wrap each ear tightly with foil and place on the grill rack over medium heat. Cook for 15 to 20 minutes, turning frequently. Remove from grill and serve. These spicy summer favorites may be grilled with their outer husks on instead of foil. Just pull back the husks, remove the corn silk threads, add butter and replace the husks for grilling.

Note: Corn factoid: Inside a corn cob there is a silk corn thread for every single kernel of corn.

Moroccan Couscous with Victoria Taylor's Moroccan Seasoning

PREPARATION TIME: 10 MINUTES / COOKING TIME: 10 MINUTES
SERVES: 4

> 1 box plain couscous
> 2 tablespoons olive oil
> 1 small onion, chopped
> 1 tablespoon Victoria Taylor's Moroccan Seasoning
> 1 large tomato, cut into ½-inch pieces
> 1 (7¾-ounce) can chick-peas, drained
> salt to taste

Cook the couscous using the package directions. Heat the olive oil in a large skillet. Sauté the onion and Moroccan Seasoning in the hot olive oil for 5 minutes. Add the tomato and chick-peas and sauté for another 2 to 3 minutes. Add cooked couscous to the chick-pea mixture and cook until heated through before serving. Season with salt to taste.

Note: There are a million variations for this recipe. Add sautéed zucchini, chopped olives, or broccoli. Use what you have in your refrigerator.

Sicilian Roasted Fennel with Bacon and Victoria Taylor's Sicilian Seasoning

PREPARATION TIME: 20 MINUTES / COOKING TIME: 45 MINUTES
SERVES: 6

4 slices bacon, cut into ½-inch strips
5 small onions
2 fennel bulbs, trimmed and quartered with green ends cut off
2 tablespoons Victoria Taylor's Sicilian Seasoning
sea salt to taste

Use an ovenproof casserole or medium high-sided saucepan for this dish. Cook the bacon until crisp and transfer it to a paper towel-covered plate to drain. Retain the bacon drippings in the pan. In a separate saucepan, add the whole onions with enough water to cover them by several inches. Bring the onions to a boil and simmer until tender, about 15 minutes. Preheat the oven to 400 degrees. Drain the onions. Now add the cooked onions, fennel, Sicilian Seasoning and bacon to the pan with the reserved bacon drippings. Transfer the pan to the oven and bake for about 45 minutes or until golden brown, stirring occasionally. Season with sea salt to taste.

Note: The combination of flavors in this dish is amazing. Fennel is such a delicious vegetable and when it's roasted it is even better.

Roasted Whole Garlic Heads with Victoria Taylor's Trapani Sea Salt

PREPARATION TIME: 5 MINUTES / COOKING TIME: 45 MINUTES
SERVES: 4

4 whole garlic heads
1/2 cup Victoria Taylor's Trapani Sea Salt
1/4 cup extra-virgin olive oil

Preheat the oven to 400 degrees. Cut the tops off the garlic heads so the cones are just exposed. Fill the bottom of a small roasting pan, such as a cake pan, with the Trapani Sea Salt. Place the garlic on the Trapani Sea Salt and drizzle with the olive oil. Cover the pan lightly with foil and bake for 45 minutes. Serve immediately.

Savory Grilled Portobello Pizzas with Victoria Taylor's Tuscan Seasoning

PREPARATION TIME: 20 MINUTES / COOKING TIME: 5 MINUTES
SERVES: 4

4 large portobello mushrooms (4 to 5 inches across)
1/2 cup olive oil, divided
2 medium tomatoes
4 teaspoons Victoria Taylor's Tuscan Seasoning
16 kalamata olives, pits removed
4 ounces feta cheese or goat cheese, crumbled

Prepare the grill for a hot fire. Remove the stems from the mushrooms. Use a spoon to scrape out the mushroom gills. Use half the olive oil (1/4 cup) to coat the mushrooms on both sides. Slice the tomatoes into 1/4-inch slices and arrange 3 slices on each Portobello Pizza. Sprinkle each pizza with 1 teaspoon Tuscan Seasoning. Slice the olives into quarters lengthwise and arrange on the pizzas and top with the crumbled cheese. Drizzle the remaining 1/4 cup olive oil over the pizzas. Place the pizzas directly over a hot fire on the grill and cover the grill. Grill for 5 minutes. Serve.

Note: The pizzas can be made up to 4 hours before grilling and kept refrigerated in a covered container. This recipe makes a great first course or the centerpiece to a vegetarian meal. The pizzas may be served on a bed of fresh arugula or baby spinach.

Spicy Home Fries with Victoria Taylor's Texas Red Seasoning

PREPARATION TIME: 10 MINUTES / COOKING TIME: 30 MINUTES
SERVES: 4

2 large red potatoes
1 1/2 tablespoons olive oil
1/2 Vidalia or other sweet onion, chopped
2 Italian-style or chicken sausages, sliced 1/2 inch thick
2 teaspoons Victoria Taylor's Texas Red Seasoning

Rinse the potatoes and remove the eyes, but do not peel. Chop into 1-inch pieces. Heat the olive oil in a heavy skillet over medium heat. Add potatoes and cook for 20 minutes or until tender when pierced with a fork, stirring occasionally. Add the onion, sausages and Texas Red Seasoning. Cook another 10 minutes or until sausage is cooked through and well blended, stirring occasionally.

Note: There are finally some excellent chicken sausages available in the market. My favorite brands are Al Fresco and Amy's Sausages. They come in a couple of varieties. Check your local market.

Roasted Provençal Potatoes with Victoria's Taylor's Herbes de Provence

PREPARATION TIME: 10 MINUTES / COOKING TIME: 50 MINUTES
SERVES: 4

1 1/2 pounds new red potatoes or red bliss potatoes
2 tablespoons light olive oil
2 tablespoons Victoria Taylor's Herbes de Provence
sea salt to taste

Preheat the oven to 425 degrees. Leave the skins on the potatoes. If the potatoes are small, cut them in half and then in half again to form wedges (3/4 to 1 inch thick). To make similar wedges with larger potatoes, cut the potatoes in half, then cut each half into 3 or 4 wedges. In a bowl or a sealable plastic bag, combine the potatoes, olive oil and Herbes de Provence. Arrange the potatoes flesh side down on a jelly roll pan or a baking sheet with a rim to keep the potatoes from falling off. Cover the pan tightly with foil and roast for 20 minutes. Remove the foil and roast for another 15 minutes. Now turn each wedge over to brown the other side and roast for a final 15 minutes. Add sea salt to taste and serve hot. The recommended red potatoes are high in moisture and low in starch. This works best for roasting. Yukon gold or all-purpose potatoes are a second choice. Potatoes with high starch and low moisture (Idaho, russet or baking potatoes) do not roast well. They tend to dry out and do not form nice light brown crusts as easily.

Note: These potatoes are frequently requested in my family. My Mediterranean Seasoning makes a great substitute for the Herbes de Provence in this recipe.

Rustic Mashed Potatoes with Victoria Taylor's Toasted Onion Herb Seasoning

PREPARATION TIME: 11 MINUTES / COOKING TIME: 20 MINUTES
SERVES: 4

　　3 large russet potatoes, unpeeled and chopped
　　2 tablespoons butter
　　2 tablespoons Victoria Taylor's Toasted Onion Herb Seasoning
　　2 tablespoons sour cream
　　1/2 cup milk

Bring enough water to cover the potatoes to a rapid boil in a pot. Add the chopped potatoes and boil until tender, about 20 minutes. Remove the pot from heat. Drain potatoes and remove from pot. In the same pot, combine the butter and Toasted Onion Herb Seasoning. Return potatoes to pot and add the sour cream and milk. Mash by hand with a potato masher or a fork to incorporate everything, but keep potatoes somewhat lumpy. Serve immediately.

Note: You may use any type of potato, like red bliss or Yukon gold potatoes, as a substitute in this recipe, but keep the skins on for more flavor.

Ratatouille with Victoria Taylor's Herbes de Provence

PREPARATION TIME: 20 MINUTES / COOKING TIME: 40 MINUTES
SERVES: 4

1 small to medium eggplant
salt to taste
1 medium zucchini
1 small yellow summer squash
1 medium onion
1 red bell pepper
1 large ripe tomato, or 8-ounce can of plum tomatoes
2 tablespoons olive oil
2 tablespoons Victoria Taylor's Herbes de Provence
2 tablespoons fresh lemon juice
pepper to taste
shaved Parmesan cheese (optional for garnish)
fresh lemon juice (optional for garnish)

Wash the eggplant and cut into 3/4-inch pieces. Sprinkle liberally with salt and place on paper towels for 20 minutes to extract bitter juices. Cut up the zucchini, squash, onion, red pepper and tomato coarsely and set aside. Heat olive oil in a sauté pan over medium heat. Rinse eggplant and pat dry. Add to sauté pan. Cook for 6 to 8 minutes to brown lightly, stirring occasionally. Add remaining vegetables, except tomato. Reduce heat. Cover and cook for 15 to 20 minutes to soften. Add chopped tomato and Herbes de Provence and cook, covered for an additional 10 minutes. Scoop vegetables from pan. Add 2 tablespoons lemon juice to pan and cook to reduce liquid until syrupy, about 5 minutes. Pour on vegetables. Season with salt and pepper to taste. Serve hot as side dish or as main course garnished with shaved cheese and fresh lemon juice.

Note: Try to take advantage of fruits and vegetables when they are in season whenever you can. I like to make this recipe in late summer when all the ingredients can be purchased fresh locally.

Italian Rice and Spinach with Victoria Taylor's Sicilian Seasoning

PREPARATION TIME: 10 MINUTES / COOKING TIME: 30 MINUTES
SERVES: 8

    1 (10-ounce) package frozen spinach
    2 cups cooked rice
    4 tablespoons butter, melted
    4 eggs, beaten
    1 cup grated Parmesan cheese
    1 cup milk
    1 small onion, chopped
    2 tablespoons Victoria Taylor's Sicilian Seasoning

Preheat the oven to 350 degrees. Cook the spinach using the package directions, then drain well. Mix the spinach, rice, butter, eggs, grated cheese, milk, onion and Sicilian Seasoning in a bowl. Spoon into a 2-quart baking dish. Bake for 30 minutes. Cut into squares to serve.

Note: For any leftovers, wrap individual servings in plastic wrap and reheat them in the microwave until warm.

Spanakopita (Spinach Pie) with Victoria Taylor's Sicilian Seasoning

PREPARATION TIME: 30 MINUTES / COOKING TIME: 45 MINUTES
SERVES: 8

filo (part of one box)
1 pound fresh spinach, cleaned and coarsely chopped
3 scallions, finely sliced
1 medium leek (pale green and white portion), cleaned and finely sliced
4 ounces cream cheese, softened
4 ounces feta cheese, finely crumbled
3 eggs
2 tablespoons Victoria Taylor's Sicilian Seasoning
light or pure olive oil (about $1/3$ cup), divided

Remove the filo from the freezer and ignore the directions on the box. Remove the filo from the box, discard the plastic covering and cover the filo with a clean, dry cloth. Preheat the oven to 425 degrees. Pat the spinach dry with a paper towel. Combine the uncooked spinach, scallions, leek, cream cheese, feta cheese, eggs, Sicilian Seasoning and 3 tablespoons of the olive oil in a bowl and mix well. Select a 9x12-inch baking pan and lightly brush the bottom with some of the remaining olive oil. Lay the filo out flat and cut 5 pieces (1 or 2 at a time) to fit the pan. One whole sheet of filo from the package is usually enough to make 2 layers in a 9x12-inch pan. Place the sheets in the pan and pat gently. Ignore any minor tears in the filo and throw away any uncooperative sheets. You have plenty. Spread half the spinach mixture on the filo and top with 1 sheet of filo. Spread the remaining spinach mixture in the pan and top with 5 more layers of filo. Brush the top of the pie lightly with the remaining olive oil. Bake for 45 minutes. It will be lightly browned on top.

Note: One of my favorite meals is Spanakopita with Sicilian Tomato, Cucumber and Feta Salad (see recipe on page 33). Both dishes are based on time-tested recipes brought to this country from Agrinion, Greece, courtesy of my best friend's grandmother.

Roasted Summer Squash with Victoria Taylor's Mediterranean Seasoning

PREPARATION TIME: 20 MINUTES / COOKING TIME: 20 MINUTES
SERVES: 6

    1 pound summer squash or zucchini
    1 tablespoon salt
    1 teaspoon olive oil
    2 teaspoons Victoria Taylor's Mediterranean Seasoning

Cut the squash in half lengthwise. Scrape out the seeds and chop into 1/2-inch pieces. Place the squash in a bowl and toss with the salt. Let rest for 15 to 20 minutes. The squash will release some of its moisture from the salt. Use a paper towel to remove as much of this moisture as possible, pressing on the squash. Preheat the oven to 475 degrees. Toss the squash with the olive oil and Mediterranean Seasoning. Arrange on a baking sheet or a jelly roll pan and roast for 20 minutes, turning once.

Note: This recipe has a few extra steps, but the squash is flavorful with a nice texture, which is a big improvement over the mushy and bland result one gets from boiling summer squash.

Chicken, Vegetarian, and Pasta Dishes

Roasted Tuscan Chicken Breasts in Orange Sauce with Victoria Taylor's Tuscan Seasoning

PREPARATION TIME: 10 MINUTES / COOKING TIME: 35 MINUTES
SERVES: 4

    4 skinless chicken breast halves
    1 tablespoon butter
    salt to taste
    1 (6-ounce) can frozen orange juice concentrate, thawed
    1 tablespoon Victoria Taylor's Tuscan Seasoning
    4 cups cooked white rice

Preheat the broiler. Place the chicken breasts on a foil-covered broiler pan. Dot with 1 tablespoon butter and broil for 5 minutes. Transfer to a baking dish just large enough to hold the chicken breasts in a single layer. Reduce oven temperature to 350 degrees. Salt the chicken, if desired. Pour the thawed orange juice concentrate over the chicken and sprinkle with the Tuscan Seasoning. Bake, uncovered, for 30 minutes. Place each chicken breast on a bed of cooked white rice and top with a spoonful of the sauce from the pan. Serve.

Note: If you forget to thaw the orange juice concentrate, just place it in a small bowl and melt it in the microwave.

Provençal Roast Chicken with Olives with Victoria Taylor's Herbes de Provence

PREPARATION TIME: 15 MINUTES / COOKING TIME: 2 TO 3 HOURS
SERVES: 3 TO 4

    1 whole chicken (3 to 4 pounds)
    olive oil
    2 to 3 tablespoons Victoria Taylor's Herbes de Provence
    sea salt and pepper to taste
    1 lemon
    1 cup mixed olives (from the cheese or deli section of your
        supermarket)

Preheat the oven to 500 degrees. Rinse chicken and pat dry. Rub entire surface with olive oil. Spread 2 to 3 tablespoons Herbes de Provence, sea salt and pepper over outside and inside of the chicken, as well as under the skin wherever you can. Roll lemon on a hard surface to release juice. Cut lemon in half and place inside chicken cavity. Place chicken on rack in roasting pan and roast for 20 minutes. Reduce oven temperature to 375 degrees and roast for an additional 40 minutes. Baste the chicken and add olives onto the rack around the chicken. If olives are too small to be caught by the rack, place some aluminum foil down on the rack and place the olives on top of the foil. Continue to roast until the internal temperature reaches 170 degrees, basting every 15 to 20 minutes. Take the chicken out of the oven and let it rest outside the oven for 10 minutes before carving. Garnish with the roasted olives. Serve with buttered bow tie pasta and fresh sautéed spinach or broccoli rabe.

Note: To get more juice from lemons, limes, and oranges, roll them on a hard surface before you cut them to extract the juice.

Moroccan Lemon Chicken with
Victoria Taylor's Moroccan Seasoning

PREPARATION TIME: 10 MINUTES / COOKING TIME: 25 MINUTES
SERVES: 4

2 tablespoons olive oil
2 large tomatoes, chopped (about 2 cups)
1/4 cup chopped green olives, pits removed (about 12 olives)
2 tablespoons Victoria Taylor's Moroccan Seasoning
1 large lemon
1 pound boneless skinless chicken breasts

Preheat the oven to 400 degrees. Heat the olive oil in a small skillet and add tomatoes, olives and Moroccan Seasoning. Sauté for 1 minute. Slice the lemon into 1/4-inch slices and arrange on the bottom of a baking dish, one slice per chicken breast. Place the chicken breasts on the lemon slices and top with the tomato mixture. Bake for 25 minutes or until chicken is cooked. Remove from oven and serve with the lemon slices as a garnish. Serve this with couscous or rice and a salad.

Note: This recipe has so much flavor from the Moroccan Seasoning, olives, and lemon slices that it works best with a plain side dish like rice or couscous, or plain buttered pasta.

Katy's Tuscan Chicken Nuggets with Victoria Taylor's Tuscan Seasoning

PREPARATION TIME: 10 MINUTES / COOKING TIME: 8 TO 10 MINUTES
SERVES: 4

    1 pound chicken cutlets
    1 egg, beaten
    1 cup plain bread crumbs
    2 tablespoons Victoria Taylor's Tuscan Seasoning
    3 tablespoons olive oil

Cut the chicken cutlets into bite-size pieces. Dip the pieces into the beaten egg, and then into a mixture of the bread crumbs and Tuscan Seasoning. Place the olive oil in a skillet over medium-high heat, then add the coated chicken to the pan. Cook for about 4 minutes or until browned on one side, then turn to brown the other side, about another 4 minutes.

Note: My good friend Katy is 7 years old. She first became addicted to Tuscan Seasoning at age 3$\frac{1}{2}$ when she tried the Tuscan Bread Dipping Oil (see recipe on page 16). The Food Network is her favorite channel. This is her recipe.

Grilled Orange Chicken with Victoria Taylor's Tuscan Seasoning

PREPARATION TIME: 10 MINUTES / COOKING TIME: 10 MINUTES
SERVES: 4

Chicken:
    4 boneless skinless chicken breasts
    2 navel oranges

Basting Mixture:
    $1/4$ cup Victoria Taylor's Tuscan Seasoning
    $3/4$ cup olive oil
    $1/4$ cup frozen orange juice concentrate

Prepare the grill for cooking with medium to high heat. Trim the chicken of any fat. Using a kitchen mallet, pound the chicken breasts to an even thickness (about $1/2$ inch). Slice the oranges into $1/4$-inch slices. Using a whisk, combine the Tuscan Seasoning, olive oil and orange juice concentrate. Use a basting brush to coat the chicken and the orange slices on both sides before grilling. Place the chicken and 8 orange slices over a medium to hot fire. Grill the chicken and the oranges for 3 minutes per side, continuing to baste occasionally while grilling. Place two grilled orange slices on each plate and top with a grilled chicken breast. Serve this savory dish with wild rice or buttered egg noodles and a salad of seasonal greens.

Note: To keep the flames to a minimum, move the chicken to the side of the grill where there is no heat and baste there before placing back on the coals. This prevents any stray drips from causing excessive flare-ups.

Chunky Chicken Chili with Victoria Taylor's Kansas City Seasoning

PREPARATION TIME: 15 MINUTES / COOKING TIME: 40 MINUTES
SERVES: 4

1 tablespoon olive or peanut oil
1 zucchini, sliced
1/2 red onion, sliced
4 ounces button mushrooms, sliced
1 pound boneless skinless chicken breast, cut into 1-inch pieces
2 tablespoons Victoria Taylor's Kansas City Seasoning
1 (8-ounce) can tomato sauce
1 (15- to 19-ounce) can red kidney beans, drained lightly
1 (11-ounce) can corn
1 teaspoon Worcestershire sauce
sour cream (optional for garnish)

Heat the olive oil in a 10- to 12-inch skillet over medium heat. Add the zucchini, onion and mushrooms to the hot oil and cook for 5 minutes. Add the chicken and cook for 6 to 8 minutes, stirring frequently. Add the Kansas City Seasoning, tomato sauce, beans, corn and Worcestershire sauce. Turn heat to low and simmer for 30 minutes. Serve over white rice with sour cream as a garnish.

Note: This recipe has whole peppercorns in it from the Kansas City Seasoning. I love coming across a bite with the earthy heat of a whole peppercorn. When you bite them, the walls of the peppercorn are crushed, releasing the volatile oils that create that great flavor signature.

Chicken and Shrimp Jambalaya with Victoria Taylor's New Orleans Seasoning

PREPARATION TIME: 45 MINUTES / COOKING TIME: 30 MINUTES
SERVES: 6

1/2 pound raw medium shrimp
2 cups water
1 teaspoon salt
2 tablespoons olive oil
1/2 large green bell pepper, cut into 1/2-inch pieces
1 small yellow onion, cut into 1/2-inch pieces
3 stalks celery, cut into 1/2-inch pieces
1/2 pound smoked ham or andouille sausage, cut into 1/2-inch pieces
1 pound boneless chicken breast, cut into 1-inch pieces
2 tablespoons Victoria Taylor's New Orleans Seasoning
1 tablespoon flour
2 cups chicken stock
1 (15-ounce) can diced tomatoes, undrained
1 (8-ounce) can tomato sauce
6 cups cooked white rice

Peel and clean shrimp and place shells and tails in a small stockpot over medium heat. Add 2 cups of water and 1 teaspoon salt. Bring to a boil. Reduce heat and simmer until reduced by half, about 20 minutes. Add the olive oil to a Dutch oven or heavy pot, and bring up to medium heat. Add green pepper, onion, celery and ham and sauté for 10 minutes or until vegetables are tender. Add chicken and brown on all sides, about 4 minutes. Add New Orleans Seasoning and cook for 1 minute. Add the flour and stir for 1 minute. Add chicken stock and stir to release any flour on the bottom of the pot. Strain shrimp stock and add to the pot. Add the tomatoes and tomato sauce. Reduce heat to low. Simmer for 30 minutes. Add the raw shrimp and cook for 3 minutes. Serve over white rice.

Note: For serving, spoon the cooked rice into individual shallow bowls, such as pasta bowls, and top with a ladleful of the Jambalaya.

Tuscan Roasted Chicken with Victoria Taylor's Tuscan Seasoning

PREPARATION TIME: 15 MINUTES / COOKING TIME: 1 HOUR
SERVES: 6

> 1 whole chicken (5- to 6-pound roaster)
> 2 to 3 tablespoons olive oil (enough to coat the bird)
> 1 lemon, cut into quarters
> 2 tablespoons Victoria Taylor's Tuscan Seasoning
>   (enough to coat the entire bird)
> salt to taste

Preheat the oven to 425 degrees. Rinse the chicken inside and out and pat dry. Rub the olive oil all over the chicken and place the lemon pieces inside the stuffing cavity. Place the chicken in a roasting pan and coat the chicken with the Tuscan Seasoning, working with your hands to loosen the skin from the chicken breast and rubbing the seasoning between the skin and the chicken breast. Season the chicken with salt to taste inside and out. Place a loose sheet of foil over the chicken and roast for 30 minutes. Remove the foil. Roast for another 30 minutes or just until cooked through. Let the chicken rest for a few minutes before cutting to serve.

Note: When serving, spoon some of the natural juices from the roasting pan onto the sliced chicken. For a quick gravy, add a mixture of 1/4 cup milk with 2 tablespoons flour to the juice and mix over medium heat. Add white wine or stock if needed to thin.

Spicy New Orleans Chicken with Victoria Taylor's New Orleans Seasoning

PREPARATION TIME: 20 MINUTES / COOKING TIME: 10 MINUTES
SERVES: 4

3/4 cup unseasoned dry bread crumbs
1 tablespoon Victoria Taylor's New Orleans Seasoning
1 pound boneless skinless chicken breasts
2 tablespoons butter
2 tablespoons olive oil
white rice

Combine the bread crumbs and New Orleans Seasoning in a large sealable plastic bag. Cut the chicken into 1-inch pieces or 1-inch-wide strips. Place chicken pieces in bread crumb mixture and shake until chicken is coated. Heat the butter and olive oil in a sauté pan until hot but not smoking. Add chicken pieces to sauté pan and cook until done, about 10 minutes. Serve with white rice. To make a spicy chicken casserole, mix with rice and beans and top with cheese.

Note: My favorite way to eat this chicken is in a spicy Caesar-style salad with chopped romaine, topped with a drizzle of blue cheese dressing.

Southwestern Fajitas with Victoria Taylor's Texas Red Seasoning

PREPARATION TIME: 1 HOUR / COOKING TIME: 15 MINUTES
SERVES: 4

    4 boneless skinless chicken breast halves
    3 tablespoons olive oil
    juice of 4 limes
    3 tablespoons Victoria Taylor's Texas Red Seasoning
    8 large flour tortillas
    1 large onion, cut into 1/2-inch strips
    1 each large green and red bell pepper, cut into 1/2-inch strips

Cut the chicken breasts into 1/2-inch strips. Combine the olive oil, lime juice and Texas Red Seasoning in a bowl and mix well. Marinate the chicken in this mixture for 30 to 60 minutes. When you are ready to cook the chicken, heat the oven to 200 degrees and place the tortillas directly on the oven rack to warm. Transfer the chicken from the marinade to a skillet, reserving the marinade. Cook the chicken over medium to high heat until done, about 5 minutes. Remove the chicken from the skillet. Add the onion, bell peppers and reserved marinade to the skillet and cook for 5 to 7 minutes or until crisp-tender, stirring constantly. Add the chicken to the skillet and stir briefly. Remove the tortillas from the oven and place them on a plate with a cover to keep them warm. Place the chicken mixture in a bowl and get ready to make fajitas!

Note: I like to let everyone make their own Fajitas. Serve them with any or all of the following in bowls so people can help themselves: sour cream, shredded Cheddar cheese, salsa, guacamole.

Curried Chicken and a Million Condiments with Victoria Taylor's Curry

PREPARATION TIME: 30 MINUTES / COOKING TIME: 40 TO 45 MINUTES
SERVES: 8

The Chicken:

3¹/₂ pounds boneless skinless chicken breasts, cut into 2-inch pieces
¹/₄ cup flour
2 tablespoons Victoria Taylor's Curry
4 tablespoons butter
¹/₄ cup olive oil
sea salt to taste

The Sauce:

2 tablespoons butter
2 medium onions, finely chopped
2 cloves garlic, minced
2 small tart apples, peeled and coarsely chopped
2 tablespoons flour
3 tablespoons Victoria Taylor's Curry
2 cups chicken broth
¹/₂ cup heavy cream
1 tablespoon lemon juice
1 tablespoon grated lemon zest

The Condiments:

shredded coconut
bacon, cooked and crumbled
cashews
scallions, thinly sliced
red onion, finely chopped
dried currants, soaked in port
sliced bananas
Major Grey's Mango Chutney
fresh avocados
golden raisins, soaked in brandy
and 999,990 others you may think of

The Chicken: Place the chicken pieces on a large foil-covered work surface near your stovetop. Combine the flour and Curry in a small bowl. Heat the butter and olive oil in a large skillet over medium heat. Coat the chicken pieces lightly with the flour mixture and transfer them in batches to the skillet. Cook the chicken just until done and lightly browned. Transfer the cooked pieces to a 2-quart baking dish. Season with sea salt to taste.

The Sauce: Add 2 tablespoons butter to the same skillet used to cook the chicken. Add the onions and sauté over medium-low heat for about 5 minutes. Add the garlic and apples and sauté until the apples are just soft enough to be mashed. Remove from heat. Combine the flour and Curry in a bowl and mix well. Add to the onion mixture. Mash the onion and apple mixture using a wooden spoon until well mixed and paste-like. Place the skillet over medium heat and add the chicken broth $1/2$ cup at a time, mixing well after each addition. Add the cream and bring the sauce to a low boil, stirring frequently. Boil for about 10 minutes, stirring frequently. The sauce should thicken quite a bit. Stir in the lemon juice and lemon zest.

Preheat the oven to 350 degrees. Pour the sauce over the chicken. Bake for 40 to 45 minutes or until heated through. Serve with plain cooked white rice and the condiments of your choice.

Note: If you like curry, don't miss this one. It's much easier than it looks and the condiments make it fun and give a different flavor and texture to every bite.

Coq Au Vin with Victoria Taylor's Herbes de Provence

PREPARATION TIME: 40 MINUTES / COOKING TIME: 1 HOUR 20 MINUTES
SERVES: 6 TO 8

6 slices thick-cut bacon, chopped
2 (3-pound) chickens, quartered
1 tablespoon olive oil
2 yellow onions, sliced
2 large carrots, chopped
3 celery stalks, chopped
1 pound button mushrooms, sliced
2 tablespoons flour
$1/4$ cup brandy or cognac
$1^1/2$ bottles red wine, such as burgundy or pinot noir
3 tablespoons Victoria Taylor's Herbes de Provence
sea salt & pepper to taste

In a deep, heavy skillet cook the bacon until done. Remove bacon from skillet. Brown the quartered chicken on all sides in bacon drippings and remove from skillet. Pour off any remaining bacon drippings. Add the olive oil and sauté onions, carrots, celery and mushrooms over medium heat until softened, about 8 minutes. Sprinkle flour over onion mixture and cook for 2 to 3 minutes, stirring frequently. Remove from heat and add brandy to the skillet. Carefully ignite with long kitchen match to burn off alcohol. Add wine and stir to mix all ingredients. Add Herbes de Provence, chicken and any accumulated juices back to skillet. Reduce heat to low. Cover and simmer for 1 hour or until chicken is cooked thoroughly. Remove chicken to serving dish and keep warm. Increase heat to medium, and simmer, uncovered, for 10 minutes to concentrate sauce. Pour sauce over chicken and serve.

Note: This recipe has incredible flavor. The combination of seasoning and ingredients is just right, and for such a fancy name, it's easy to prepare.

Curried Macaroni and Cheese with Victoria Taylor's Curry

PREPARATION: 30 MINUTES / COOKING TIME: 30 MINUTES
SERVES: 6

8 ounces elbow macaroni, cooked
1 tablespoon cornstarch
1 1/2 teaspoons dry mustard, divided
1 1/2 teaspoons Victoria Taylor's Curry, divided
1/2 cup (1 stick) butter, divided
2 cups milk (whole milk or 2 percent)
2 full cups grated sharp Cheddar cheese
1/2 teaspoon salt
1/2 teaspoon pepper
2 1/2 cups bread crumbs torn from fresh white bread
    (French or sourdough)

Preheat the oven to 350 degrees. Cook and drain the macaroni. Use a square 8- or 9-inch baking dish or pan for this recipe. Combine the cornstarch, 1 teaspoon of the dry mustard and 1 teaspoon of the Curry in a large saucepan. Add 3 tablespoons of the butter. Cook and whisk until mixed. Now add the milk, stirring constantly. Continue to cook until sauce thickens and boils, about 5 minutes. Remove from heat. Add the grated cheese, salt and pepper and whisk until smooth. Stir in the cooked macaroni and transfer to the baking dish. To prepare the bread crumbs, melt the remaining butter in a large skillet until hot but not burning. Mix in the remaining 1/2 teaspoon dry mustard and 1/2 teaspoon Curry. Add the bread crumbs and cook on medium to low heat until crispy and golden brown, about 8 minutes, stirring constantly. Sprinkle the bread crumbs over the macaroni and bake for 30 minutes or until bubbling at the edges. Serve.

Note: If you have ever had real homemade mac and cheese, you know it's worth it. I'm a so-called "gourmet," but my favorite foods are mac and cheese and grilled cheese sandwiches.

Vegetable Chili with Victoria Taylor's Texas Red Seasoning

PREPARATION TIME: 20 MINUTES / COOKING TIME: 50 MINUTES
SERVES: 8

1/2 cup olive oil, divided
2 zucchini, cut into 1/2-inch dice
2 onions, cut into 1/2-inch dice
6 cloves garlic, finely chopped
1 green and 1 red bell pepper, cut into 1/4-inch pieces
1 (35-ounce) can plum tomatoes, undrained
1 1/2 pounds plum tomatoes, cut into 1-inch pieces
1/2 cup chopped fresh Italian parsley
1/4 cup (or more) Victoria Taylor's Texas Red Seasoning
1 teaspoon salt
1 small can red kidney beans, drained
1 small can chick-peas, drained
3 tablespoons fresh lemon juice
1/4 cup chopped fresh dill
Toppings: sour cream, grated Cheddar cheese and chopped red onions

Heat 1/4 cup of the olive oil in a large skillet until hot but not smoking. Sauté the zucchini until tender, about 5 minutes. Transfer the zucchini to a large flameproof casserole. Heat the remaining 1/4 cup olive oil in the skillet. Sauté the onions, garlic and bell peppers for 10 minutes. Add them to the casserole. Now heat the casserole over low to medium heat and add the canned and fresh tomatoes, parsley, Texas Red Seasoning and salt. Simmer, uncovered, for 30 minutes. Add the beans, chick-peas, lemon juice and fresh dill. Simmer for another 20 minutes. Serve in bowls with any or all of the toppings.

Note: This is such a filling and satisfying chili, even though a vegetarian chili is somewhat of a contradiction. I serve this chili with bread only. A salad is not really needed. My very best friend, Alex Marren, makes this recipe at least twice a month.

Sliced Tomato and Goat Cheese Pizza with Victoria Taylor's Sicilian Seasoning

PREPARATION TIME: 10 MINUTES / COOKING TIME: 10 TO 12 MINUTES
SERVES: 4 (2 SLICES PER PERSON FROM A 12-INCH PIZZA)

    refrigerated pizza dough for one 12-inch pizza
    1½ cups canned crushed tomatoes (½ of a 28-ounce can)
    1 tablespoon Victoria Taylor's Sicilian Seasoning
    2 medium tomatoes, thinly sliced
    ½ cup crumbled goat cheese or feta cheese

The Cooking Surface: There are several options here. The key is to make sure the bottom of the crust gets cooked. Pizza stones or pizza tiles work well because they are heated in the oven before the pizza is cooked, so the dough goes immediately onto a very hot surface. If you use a pizza tile or stone, you will need a pizza paddle to transfer the pizza from your work surface to the oven. I use a 14-inch pan with small holes in it. This works well too because the holes help to crisp the dough. Another very effective option for a cooking surface is the top of your broiler pan, which has a pattern of holes or slits in it. Remove the top of your broiler pan and use it as you would a pizza pan. If you use a broiler pan, spray it with nonstick cooking spray.

The Pizza: Preheat the oven to 550 degrees. Shape the pizza dough on your work surface or on the pan with your hands by pulling and stretching it. Combine the crushed tomatoes and Sicilian Seasoning in a bowl and mix well. Spread the sauce evenly over the dough. Cover with the tomato slices. Sprinkle with the crumbled cheese. Bake for 10 to 12 minutes. Remove from oven. Let stand for 2 to 3 minutes before slicing.

Popeye and Olive Oil Go to Tuscany with Victoria Taylor's Tuscan Seasoning

PREPARATION TIME: 10 MINUTES / COOKING TIME: 15 MINUTES
SERVES: 4

  1 pound penne or bow tie pasta
  1 tablespoon sea salt
  1 box frozen spinach, or 1 pound fresh spinach
  1 medium onion, chopped
  3 tablespoons olive oil
  1 (15-ounce) can diced tomatoes
  2 tablespoons Victoria Taylor's Tuscan Seasoning
  shredded mozzarella and Parmesan cheese (optional)

Cook the pasta in a large pot with the sea salt while you prepare the sauce. Cook the frozen or fresh spinach and set aside. Sauté the chopped onion in the olive oil in a skillet for about 5 minutes. Add the can of tomatoes and Tuscan Seasoning and sauté for another 3 minutes. When the pasta is done, toss with the tomato mixture and cooked spinach. Sprinkle with shredded cheeses and serve.

Note: I try very hard to use freshly grated Parmigiano-Reggiano cheese whenever Parmesan cheese is called for. My favorite magazine, *Cooks Illustrated*, recently confirmed what I already knew: Parmigiano-Reggiano is absolutely the best and worth the few extra minutes.

Pasta with Arugula, Prosciutto and Parmesan with Victoria Taylor's Tuscan Seasoning

PREPARATION TIME: 20 MINUTES / COOKING TIME: 10 MINUTES
SERVES: 4

1 pound linguini, spaghetti or penne
1 tablespoon sea salt
3 tablespoons olive oil
1 medium onion, coarsely chopped
1 cup diced red bell pepper
1 cup sliced button mushrooms
1 cup sliced summer squash or zucchini
1 chopped tomato ($1/2$ of a 14-ounce can diced tomatoes)
2 tablespoons Victoria Taylor's Tuscan Seasoning
$1/4$ cup white wine
1 (4-ounce) bag fresh arugula
$1/4$ pound prosciutto, cut into 1-inch pieces
$1/2$ cup grated Parmesan cheese
1 to 2 tablespoons butter (optional)
grated nutmeg (optional for garnish)
fresh lemon juice from 1 lemon (optional for garnish)

Begin by bringing a large pot of water to a boil. Add pasta and sea salt to water. Cook using the package directions. Drain in a colander, reserving $1/4$ cup of the pasta water to make sauce. Meanwhile, heat the olive oil in pan and add onion, red pepper, mushrooms and summer squash. Cook vegetables for about 5 minutes, then add tomato and Tuscan Seasoning. Cook for 3 minutes and add wine, bringing to a boil. Add arugula and prosciutto and cook for 2 minutes. Add grated cheese and reserved pasta water, which will lend body to the sauce. Swirl butter into sauce. Serve atop pasta and garnish with some grated nutmeg and fresh lemon juice.

Tuscany Chicken over Bow Tie Pasta with Victoria Taylor's Tuscan Seasoning

PREPARATION TIME: 15 MINUTES / COOKING TIME: 30 MINUTES
SERVES: 4

4 boneless skinless chicken breast halves
2 tablespoons olive oil
3 tablespoons Victoria Taylor's Tuscan Seasoning, divided
1 (28-ounce) can diced tomatoes with juice
1 teaspoon salt
1/3 cup grated mozzarella cheese
4 servings cooked bow tie pasta

Preheat the oven to 350 degrees. Slice the chicken breasts in half horizontally to create 8 thin cutlets. Use a 9x12-inch Pyrex baking dish or pan for this recipe. Coat the bottom of the pan with the olive oil. Sprinkle 1 tablespoon of the Tuscan Seasoning on the bottom of the dish. Place the chicken cutlets in the pan, overlapping them as little as possible. Pour the diced tomatoes over the chicken and sprinkle with the remaining Tuscan Seasoning and the salt. Now sprinkle the grated cheese on top and bake for 30 minutes or just until the chicken is cooked. While the chicken is baking, cook and drain the pasta. Serve the pasta on a plate and top each serving with two pieces of chicken and some of the cooking juice. Garnish with additional grated cheese.

Note: This is a quick and easy dish for family or friends. Other kinds of cheese, such as Cheddar or Parmesan, may be substituted for the mozzarella, if desired. Serve with salad and bread.

Tuscan Penne Pasta and Sesame Chicken with Victoria Taylor's Tuscan Seasoning

PREPARATION: 20 MINUTES / COOKING TIME: 15 MINUTES
SERVES: 4

  3 tablespoons toasted sesame oil
  1 medium onion, chopped
  5 teaspoons Victoria Taylor's Tuscan Seasoning
  2 large boneless skinless chicken breasts, cut into 1-inch pieces
  1 (14-ounce) can diced tomatoes
  4 to 5 cups penne
  1 tablespoon sea salt

Heat the sesame oil in a large skillet until hot but not smoking. Add the onion and sauté for 2 minutes, then stir in the Tuscan Seasoning. Add the chicken and sauté just until cooked through. Add the tomatoes and bring the mixture to a low simmer. Bring a medium saucepan of water to a boil to cook the pasta. Add the pasta and sea salt. Boil until the pasta is cooked firm, but not too soft. Now drain the pasta and add to the skillet with the chicken and tomatoes. Simmer over low heat for 5 minutes before serving to allow the pasta to absorb some of the liquid from the skillet.

Note: Tuscan Seasoning is my bestseller, and it happens to be salt free, because I just didn't think it needed any salt when I developed it. So for Tuscan pasta dishes, you will need a good quality sea salt in the pasta water to enhance the flavor of the pasta.

Pasta with Chard, Braised Fennel and Grape Tomatoes and Victoria Taylor's Herbes de Provence

PREPARATION TIME: 20 MINUTES / COOKING TIME: 40 MINUTES
SERVES: 4

1 medium onion, thinly sliced
1/4 cup olive oil
1 medium-large fennel bulb, trimmed and thinly sliced
(reserve 2 tablespoons finely chopped fennel fronds, optional for
    garnish)
3 cloves garlic, minced
3/4 cup water
2 1/2 tablespoons balsamic vinegar
1 tablespoon Victoria Taylor's Herbes de Provence
1/4 teaspoon crushed red pepper flakes
1 1/2 cups grape tomatoes, sliced lengthwise (Santa brand grape
    tomatoes preferred)
1 pound spaghetti
4 quarts water
2 tablespoons sea salt
1 large bunch chard (any variety), coarsely chopped
3/4 cup grated Parmigiano-Reggiano

For the Braised Fennel and Grape Tomatoes: Sauté the onion in
the olive oil in a skillet over medium heat for about 5 minutes. Add
the fennel and garlic and sauté an additional 10 minutes until slightly
browned, stirring frequently. Add 3/4 cup water and simmer, partially
covered, for 8 to 10 minutes or until the liquid is evaporated. Stir in the
balsamic vinegar, Herbes de Provence, pepper flakes and tomatoes
and simmer for an additional 2 minutes.

For the Pasta and Chard: Boil the pasta in 4 quarts water in a saucepan with 2 tablespoons sea salt for 6 minutes. Add the chard to the pasta water and boil for an additional 5 minutes. Drain the pasta and chard mixture gently (don't drain too thoroughly as pasta may be too dry). Combine the pasta with the fennel and tomato mixture and toss with the grated cheese. Garnish with chopped fennel fronds and serve with additional grated cheese, if desired.

Note: Always salt your pasta water with a good quality sea salt before cooking. It imparts a wonderful flavor that is far more satisfying than salting the finished dish.

Classic Sicilian Red Sauce with Victoria Taylor's Sicilian Seasoning

PREPARATION TIME: 5 MINUTES / COOKING TIME: 15 MINUTES
SERVES: 4 AS A SAUCE FOR PASTA

  1 (28-ounce) can crushed tomatoes (Hunt's® preferred)
  5 teaspoons Victoria Taylor's Sicilian Seasoning
  1 tablespoon extra-virgin olive oil
  sea salt to taste

Combine the undrained tomatoes, Sicilian Seasoning, olive oil and sea salt in a saucepan and simmer for 15 minutes before serving over pasta. Mediterranean Seasoning is a good substitute for the Sicilian Seasoning in this recipe.

Note: This recipe is so easy, but the flavor is amazing. I use it simply for pasta or as the base for any recipe calling for red sauce.

Seafood

Cajun Cornmeal Catfish with Victoria Taylor's New Orleans Seasoning

PREPARATION TIME: 10 MINUTES / COOKING TIME: 11 TO 13 MINUTES
SERVES: 4

1½ pounds freshwater catfish fillets
1 cup cornmeal
2 tablespoons peanut oil
1 to 2 tablespoons Victoria Taylor's New Orleans Seasoning
salt and pepper to taste
lemons (optional for garnish)

Rinse catfish and pat dry. Spread cornmeal over a large plate. Heat peanut oil in a well-seasoned cast-iron skillet or other heavy gauge pan over medium heat. Sprinkle both sides of the catfish with a generous amount of New Orleans Seasoning and coat with the cornmeal. Fry in skillet for 5 to 6 minutes and flip. Cook for an additional 6 to 7 minutes or until cooked all the way through. Season with salt and pepper to taste. Garnish with lemons. Serve with rice and corn.

Note: Always buy the freshest fish you can get. Ask the salesperson about the freshness of the fish and where it came from.

Baked Cod and Chunky Tomato Sauce with Victoria Taylor's Seafood Seasoning

PREPARATION TIME: 15 MINUTES / COOKING TIME: 25 MINUTES
SERVES: 4

1/4 cup flour
1/4 cup Victoria Taylor's Seafood Seasoning, divided
2 tablespoons peanut oil
2 tablespoons butter
1 1/2 pounds fresh cod, cut into 2-inch pieces
1 (28-ounce) can diced tomatoes
2 tablespoons lemon juice
salt to taste

Preheat the oven to 400 degrees. Mix the flour with 2 tablespoons of the Seafood Seasoning. Heat peanut oil and butter until hot but not smoking in a large ovenproof skillet. Coat the cut pieces of cod in the flour mixture and sear them in the skillet until golden on both sides, about 8 minutes per side. Combine the tomatoes, lemon juice and remaining Seafood Seasoning in a bowl and mix well. Pour over the fish. Transfer the skillet to the oven and bake until fish is white throughout, about 10 minutes. Serve, adding salt to taste.

Note: Other kinds of fish may be substituted very successfully for cod here. The only caution is to avoid fillets which may be too thin or delicate to sear on both sides, such as sole.

Baked Flounder with Victoria Taylor's Holiday Seasoning

PREPARATION TIME: 10 MINUTES / COOKING TIME: 6 TO 8 MINUTES
SERVES: 4 TO 6

1¹/₂ pounds flounder or sole fillets
olive oil to coat pan
2 tablespoons dry vermouth
1 to 2 tablespoons Victoria Taylor's Holiday Seasoning
salt and pepper to taste
lemon wedges

Preheat the oven to 325 degrees. Rinse the fillets and pat dry. Arrange on a lightly oiled baking pan. Sprinkle fillets with vermouth, Holiday Seasoning and salt and pepper to taste. Bake on top rack in oven until fish turns opaque throughout, about 6 to 8 minutes. Remove from oven and serve with some fresh lemon wedges, buttered pasta and a simple green salad.

Note: This is a great example of a simple recipe that shines with the addition of the seasoning. You won't believe such a simple and easy recipe can be so flavorful.

Lemon Flounder with Victoria Taylor's Seafood Seasoning

PREPARATION TIME: 10 MINUTES / COOKING TIME: 15 MINUTES
SERVES: 4

1 1/2 pounds flounder fillets
2 thin slices of fresh lemon for each fillet
2 tablespoons Victoria Taylor's Seafood Seasoning
   (enough to generously coat 1/2 of the lemon slices)
2 tablespoons butter

Preheat the oven to 425 degrees. Rinse the fillets under cool water and pat dry with a paper towel. Generously coat half the lemon slices with Seafood Seasoning. Fold each fillet in half and place a Seafood Seasoning-coated lemon slice inside each fillet like a sandwich. Place the fillets on a greased baking pan or dish. Top each folded fillet with a plain slice of lemon and dot with butter. Bake for 15 minutes or until fish is white throughout.

Note: In seasonings, the larger the pieces of herbs and spices the better. The coarse texture retains more of the naturally occurring volatile oils, i.e., more flavor.

South Side Mahimahi Salad with Orange Blossom Marinade and Victoria Taylor's Curry

PREPARATION TIME: 30 MINUTES
REFRIGERATION TIME: 4 HOURS / COOKING TIME: 30 MINUTES
SERVES: 4

Salad:
2 teaspoons grated orange rind
1/4 cup dark rum
1 medium sweet orange, peeled and sectioned
6 dried purple plums, chopped and soaked
4 cups seasonal greens
2 ounces goat cheese
4 slices bacon, cooked and broken into pieces
1/4 cup plain bread crumbs
1 tablespoon Victoria Taylor's Curry
1 pound mahimahi, grilled (3 to 4 ounces per person)
1 tablespoon peanut oil

Bermuda Onion Sauté and Marinade Dressing:
2 tablespoons multi-floral orange blossom honey
1 tablespoon unsalted butter
1/4 cup orange juice
1/4 cup dark rum
1 Bermuda onion (or other sweet onion), thinly sliced
lemon and orange slices (optional for garnish)

For the Salad: Combine the grated orange rind, dark rum, orange sections and chopped purple plums in a bowl. Allow to macerate for 4 hours or more. Stir once. Drain. Arrange greens on four salad plates. Portion goat cheese on each plate. Sprinkle with bacon pieces and refrigerate. Prepare the grill for cooking. Mix bread crumbs with Curry. Coat mahimahi with peanut oil and rub fish with bread crumb mixture. Grill fish until opaque and break into pieces. Keep warm.

For the Bermuda Onion Sauté and Marinade Dressing: In a large sauté pan, heat together the honey, butter, orange juice and rum. Add the sliced onion and cook until well glazed with the sauce, spooning sauce over the top and rolling the tasty onions around until softened. Top the salad greens with the cooked fish and dress the salad with the onion mixture. (Use additional orange juice if sauce needs to be thinned for marinade dressing.) Garnish with lemon and orange slices.

Note: I love Curry and fruit in a recipe. The sweetness of the Curry brings out the citrus notes in this recipe.

Baked Breaded Haddock with Victoria Taylor's Tuscan Seasoning

PREPARATION TIME: 5 MINUTES / COOKING TIME: 15 MINUTES
SERVES: 4

2/3 cup unseasoned dry bread crumbs
2 tablespoons Victoria Taylor's Tuscan Seasoning
1 teaspoon grated Parmesan cheese
1/2 teaspoon sea salt
1 1/2 pounds haddock or cod fillets
1 tablespoon butter
lemon wedges

Preheat the oven to 350 degrees. Mix the bread crumbs, Tuscan Seasoning, grated cheese and sea salt in a small bowl. Rinse fish and pat dry. Place fillets on an oiled baking pan and top with the bread crumb mixture. Slice the butter into thin pats and place on top of fillets. Bake in oven until golden brown and fish underneath is cooked throughout, about 15 minutes. Serve with lemon wedges.

Broiled Salmon Fillets with Victoria Taylor's Seafood Seasoning

PREPARATION TIME: 5 MINUTES / COOKING TIME: 10 MINUTES
SERVES: 4

1 1/2 pounds salmon fillets
2 tablespoons olive oil
2 tablespoons Victoria Taylor's Seafood Seasoning
1 lemon wedge
salt to taste

Preheat the broiler to high. Rinse the salmon under cool water and pat dry with a paper towel. Place the salmon skin side down on a foil-covered broiler pan or baking sheet. Moisten the salmon with the olive oil, then coat it with the Seafood Seasoning. Broil, watching carefully, for 10 minutes or longer for a thick fillet. Squeeze the lemon wedge on the salmon before serving and add salt to taste.

Note: Salmon is a rich and flavorful fish, so I like to serve it with white or brown rice and a seasonal veggie.

Mediterranean Baked Sole with
Victoria Taylor's Mediterranean Seasoning

PREPARATION TIME: 15 MINUTES / COOKING TIME: 15 MINUTES
SERVES: 4

    4 tablespoons butter, divided
    2 large tomatoes, chopped
    5 teaspoons Victoria Taylor's Mediterranean Seasoning
    2 tablespoons grated Parmesan cheese
    1 1/2 pounds sole fillets
    lemon wedges (optional for garnish)
    sea salt to taste (optional for garnish)

Preheat the oven to 375 degrees. Melt 3 tablespoons of the butter in a skillet. Add the chopped tomatoes and Mediterranean Seasoning and sauté for 30 seconds. Remove from heat and stir in the grated cheese. Arrange the fish on a buttered 9x12-inch baking dish or pan. Coat half of each fillet with the tomato mixture and fold the other half over on top of the half that has been coated. Dot the folded fillets with the remaining butter. Bake for 15 minutes. Garnish with lemon wedges and sea salt to taste.

Note: The first time I cooked this, two people who claimed that they did not like fish were fighting over the last fillet. Don't skimp on the butter.

Sicilian Grilled Swordfish with Victoria Taylor's Sicilian Seasoning

PREPARATION TIME: 25 MINUTES / COOKING TIME: 15 MINUTES
SERVES: 4

1¹/₂ pounds swordfish steaks, cut into 4 pieces
2 tablespoons Victoria Taylor's Sicilian Seasoning
¹/₄ cup olive oil
2 lemons
salt and pepper to taste
12 kalamata olives (optional for garnish)

Prepare charcoal grill and bring temperature to medium-high. Rinse the swordfish and pat dry with paper towels. Mix the Sicilian Seasoning and olive oil in a small bowl. Roll one lemon firmly on a hard surface, which will make it easier to juice. Rinse outside and remove zest with a zester or paring knife and add to the olive oil mixture, along with all the juice from that lemon. Add salt and pepper to taste and let stand for 15 to 20 minutes. Cut remaining lemon into 4 thick slices, discarding ends. Brush olive oil mixture on one side of swordfish and place that side down to grill. Grill for 6 to 8 minutes or until juice begins to collect on top side, and bottom side appears cooked. Brush most of remaining olive oil mixture on the uncooked side and flip over. Cook for 5 minutes. Coat lemon disks with the last of the olive oil mixture and grill for 2 minutes. Flip and grill for 2 more minutes and remove from grill. Check swordfish for doneness and remove when cooked through. Top each swordfish steak with a grilled lemon slice and 3 kalamata olives.

Note: The olives in this recipe are optional, but they add such a great flavor to the dish. Use capers as a substitute, if desired.

Smothered Texas Swordfish Steaks with Victoria Taylor's Texas Red Seasoning

PREPARATION TIME: 10 MINUTES / COOKING TIME: 10 MINUTES
SERVES: 4

1 tablespoon olive oil
1 red, orange or yellow bell pepper, sliced
1 medium onion, sliced
1/2 pound button mushrooms, sliced
4 scallions, sliced, green tops reserved
4 swordfish steaks (6 to 8 ounces)
1 to 2 tablespoons Victoria Taylor's Texas Red Seasoning
salt and pepper to taste

Preheat the broiler. Heat olive oil in a sauté pan. Sauté bell pepper, onion, mushrooms and white part of scallions in the hot olive oil until tender. Meanwhile, rinse swordfish and pat dry. Spread the Texas Red Seasoning over the swordfish on a broiling pan and broil until fish is cooked, about 10 minutes. Transfer swordfish to serving plates and top with the sautéed vegetables and reserved green scallion tops. Serve with wild rice and spicy black beans.

Note: I always buy fresh swordfish. If I can't get it, I substitute another fresh fish. Frozen swordfish has a chewy and dry character, not nearly as good as fresh.

Tangy Tuna Burgers with Victoria Taylor's New Orleans Seasoning

PREPARATION TIME: 30 MINUTES / COOKING TIME: 10 MINUTES
SERVES: 4

The Burgers:
1 1/2 pounds fresh tuna
4 large cloves garlic, minced
3 tablespoons Dijon mustard
1 tablespoon Victoria Taylor's New Orleans Seasoning

The Sauce:
1/3 cup teriyaki sauce
2 teaspoons minced ginger
3 cloves garlic, minced
1 tablespoon honey
1 tablespoon mustard
1/2 teaspoon white vinegar

For the Burgers: Use a large sharp knife to chop the tuna very finely until it resembles course ground beef. Combine the tuna with the minced garlic, Dijon mustard and New Orleans Seasoning. Shape the burgers.

For the Sauce: Combine the teriyaki sauce, ginger, garlic, honey, mustard and vinegar in a small bowl and whisk to mix well. Prepare the grill for cooking with high heat. Grill the burgers over high heat for about 5 minutes per side and serve on rolls with the sauce.

Note: This recipe was inspired by a lunchtime menu favorite at the Union Square Cafe in New York City. Some skeptics have been heard to say; "Isn't this recipe like using filet mignon to make hamburgers?" All I can say is indulge and taste for yourself.

White Fish Fillets and Herb Bread Crumbs with Victoria Taylor's Herbes de Provence

PREPARATION TIME: 20 MINUTES / COOKING TIME: 6 MINUTES
SERVES: 4

    1/2 cup fine dry bread crumbs
    2 tablespoons Victoria Taylor's Herbes de Provence
    1 to 1 1/2 pounds white fish fillets, such as cod, sole, haddock
    2 tablespoons butter
    lemon wedges

Combine the bread crumbs and Herbes de Provence in a bowl and mix well. Coat each fillet with the bread crumb mixture. Heat 1/2 of the butter in a large skillet and cook 1/2 of the fillets over medium heat for about 3 minutes per side or until golden brown and the fillets are just cooked. Repeat with the remaining butter and fillets. Sprinkle with lemon just before serving.

Note: I like to serve this dish on a large plate with a lemon wedge garnish. White fish works well with almost any seasonal vegetable and rice or baked or roasted potatoes.

Pecan-Crusted White Fish with Rémoulade Sauce and Victoria Taylor's New Orleans Seasoning

PREPARATION TIME: 35 MINUTES / COOKING TIME: 8 TO 10 MINUTES
SERVES: 4

The Fish:

1 pound white fish fillets, such as red snapper, cod, flounder, grouper or orange roughy, $^1/_2$ inch thick
2 tablespoons olive oil
2 teaspoons Victoria Taylor's New Orleans Seasoning
1 tablespoon butter
$^1/_2$ cup pecans, chopped
2 tablespoons chopped fresh Italian parsley

The Rémoulade Sauce:

$^1/_4$ cup Dijon mustard
$^1/_4$ cup mayonnaise
2 tablespoons honey
1 tablespoon lemon juice
$^1/_2$ red bell pepper
$^1/_4$ cup chopped scallions (white and light green parts only)
1 tablespoon minced shallots
2 tablespoons fresh Italian parsley, chopped

For the Fish: For this dish, I use parchment paper to line a baking sheet, but foil may be substituted as a liner. Rinse the fillets in cool water and pat dry. Divide the fillets into 4 servings before cooking. Place them on the lined baking sheet, skin side down. Combine the olive oil with the New Orleans Seasoning in a bowl and mix well. Brush a light coating of the mixture onto the fish. In a sauté pan, melt the butter on medium heat and toast the chopped pecans for 4 minutes, stirring frequently. Remove the pecans from the pan and let cool for several minutes in a small bowl before combining them with the 2 tablespoons of chopped fresh parsley. This is a good time to make the rémoulade sauce.

For the Rémoulade Sauce: Combine the Dijon mustard, mayonnaise, honey, lemon juice, red pepper, scallions, shallots and parsley in a food processor and pulse until the red pepper and scallions are finely chopped. Set aside. Preheat the oven to 400 degrees. Now press the pecan-parsley mix onto the fillets. Bake for 8 to 10 minutes for 1/2-inch-thick fillets, less for thinner fillets. The fish should be cooked just until opaque when done. Serve immediately with a spoonful of the rémoulade sauce.

Note: This is an easy dish with minimal preparation time. The Rémoulade Sauce may be made ahead to save time. It keeps well in the refrigerator for up to 3 days.

Greek Isles Crispy Fried Fish Fillets with Victoria Taylor's Mediterranean Seasoning

PREPARATION TIME: 10 MINUTES / COOKING TIME: 10 MINUTES
SERVES: 4

1 cup peanut or canola oil
1½ pounds haddock or cod fillets
4 teaspoons Victoria Taylor's Mediterranean Seasoning
1 cup flour
1 teaspoon baking powder
2 eggs, beaten lightly
lemon wedges (optional for garnish)
sea salt and pepper to taste

Heat the peanut oil until hot but not smoking in a 10- to 12-inch skillet. Coat one side of fish with the Mediterranean Seasoning. Mix flour and baking powder thoroughly and spread on a dinner plate. Dip fillets into beaten eggs and coat with flour mixture on both sides. Place in hot oil making sure not to crowd the skillet. Cook on one side for 5 to 7 minutes or until edges appear golden brown, then flip with spatula. Cook for an additional 3 to 4 minutes or until golden brown on the bottom. Remove from skillet and place on paper towel-lined plate to drain. Garnish with fresh lemon wedges. Season with sea salt and pepper to taste. Serve with white rice and sautéed spinach.

Note: Always salt to taste with a good quality sea salt. Everyone's palate craves salt differently. Use your own taste as a guide.

Grilled Fish Steaks with Cherry Tomatoes with Victoria Taylor's Seafood Seasoning

PREPARATION TIME: 10 MINUTES / COOKING TIME: 14 MINUTES
SERVES: 4

The Fish:
2 pounds swordfish, tuna or salmon steaks
3 tablespoons olive oil
3 tablespoons Victoria Taylor's Seafood Seasoning
25 to 30 cherry or grape tomatoes

Basting Mixture:
3 tablespoons olive oil
1 tablespoon red wine vinegar
1 tablespoon Victoria Taylor's Seafood Seasoning
1 teaspoon salt

For the Fish: Prepare the grill for cooking with medium to high heat. Rinse the fish steaks in water and pat dry. Rub the fish steaks first with 3 tablespoons olive oil then rub with 3 tablespoons Seafood Seasoning. Thread the tomatoes onto 2 or 3 grilling skewers.

For the Basting Mixture: Combine the olive oil, vinegar, Seafood Seasoning and salt in a bowl. Place the fish steaks and the skewered tomatoes on the grill over medium to high heat. Baste the tomatoes and fish steaks occasionally with the mixture while grilling for 7 minutes per side.

Note: Serve the grilled fish steaks and tomatoes with cucumber slices and feta cheese.

Herb-Crusted Fish Steaks with Victoria Taylor's Seafood Seasoning

PREPARATION TIME: 10 MINUTES / COOKING TIME: 10 TO 12 MINUTES
SERVES: 4

1/4 cup olive oil, divided
4 fish steaks, such as halibut, tuna or swordfish
1/4 cup Victoria Taylor's Seafood Seasoning
salt and pepper to taste
8 large cremini mushrooms
lemon wedges (optional)

Preheat the broiler. Coat ovenproof pan with 2 tablespoons of the olive oil. Arrange the fish steaks in the pan and flip to coat with olive oil. Coat each fish steak with the Seafood Seasoning and salt and pepper to taste on both sides and place back in pan. Coat mushrooms with the remaining olive oil and arrange around fish steaks in pan. Place pan 4 to 6 inches below broiler. Broil for 10 to 12 minutes or until fish steaks are opaque throughout, turning once. Serve with lemon wedges.

Note: I like to serve this dish on a large plate with a lemon wedge garnish. Fish steaks work well with almost any seasonal vegetable and rice or baked or roasted potatoes.

Fisherman's Stew with Victoria Taylor's Seafood Seasoning

PREPARATION TIME: 15 MINUTES / COOKING TIME: 1 HOUR
SERVES: 4

1 pound cod fillets
12 littleneck or cherrystone clams
1/3 pound small, uncooked shrimp
2 large russet potatoes, quartered
1 tablespoon olive oil
1/2 pound chorizo or linguica
1 medium onion, roughly chopped
3 tablespoons Victoria Taylor's Seafood Seasoning
3/4 cup white wine
2 bottles (8 ounces) of clam juice with 1 cup of water
1/3 pound scallops
1/4 cup orange juice
1/4 cup tomato paste
fresh cilantro or fresh flat-leaf parsley and lemon wedges
    (optional for garnish)

Rinse the fish fillets and clams. Peel and devein the shrimp, leaving tails on. Boil the potatoes in enough water to cover in a saucepan until tender, about 20 minutes. In a very large skillet or Dutch oven, heat olive oil over medium heat and add chorizo and onion. Sauté for 10 minutes. Add the Seafood Seasoning and white wine and cook for 1 minute. Add clam juice with 1 cup water and bring to boil. Add clams and cover. Cook until they all open, about 8 minutes. (Discard any clams that do not open.) Remove clams from skillet and set aside. Add the potatoes and fish fillets and cook, covered, for about 4 minutes. Add the shrimp and scallops and cook for 2 minutes or until seafood is cooked through. With a slotted spoon evenly divide cooked stew and clams into 4 serving bowls. Stir the orange juice and tomato paste into the remaining liquid in the skillet. Cook to reduce slightly, about 5 minutes. Ladle stock into serving bowls, dividing equally. Garnish with fresh cilantro and lemon wedges.

Linguini and Red Clam Sauce with Victoria Taylor's Sicilian Seasoning

PREPARATION: 15 MINUTES / COOKING TIME: 10 TO 15 MINUTES
SERVES: 4

1 pound linguini
1 to 2 tablespoons olive oil
1/2 medium onion, chopped
1 (14-ounce) can tomatoes with juices, chopped
1/2 cup white wine
2 tablespoons Victoria Taylor's Sicilian Seasoning
2 tablespoons tomato paste
2 (6-ounce) cans clams
salt and pepper to taste
grated Parmesan cheese (optional for garnish)

Bring a large pot of water to a boil to cook pasta. Heat olive oil in a sauté pan over medium heat. Add onion and sauté for 5 minutes to soften. Add tomatoes with juices, wine, Sicilian Seasoning and tomato paste and mix well. Simmer for 5 minutes. Add juice from clams and simmer for 10 to 15 minutes longer to reduce. Cook pasta while sauce reduces. When pasta is just about cooked, add clams and 2 tablespoons pasta water to sauce. Drain pasta and serve with sauce. Garnish with grated cheese.

Note: Canned tomatoes are amazingly good. The color is usually a nice dark red and the flavor is surprisingly fresh. I find that Hunt's® brand canned tomatoes are consistently good and better than the expensive, imported brands.

Simmering Cajun Shrimp with Victoria Taylor's New Orleans Seasoning

PREPARATION TIME: 15 MINUTES / COOKING TIME: 12 MINUTES
SERVES: 4

    1 (12-ounce) bottle dark beer
    2 tablespoons Victoria Taylor's New Orleans Seasoning
    2 cups light cream
    1 1/2 pounds shrimp, shelled, cleaned and tails removed

Use a large skillet for this dish. Combine beer and New Orleans Seasoning in skillet and cook until the mixture becomes very thick, stirring constantly. Add the cream gradually while stirring. Simmer for 10 minutes, stirring occasionally. Add shrimp and cook for 2 to 3 minutes. Remove from heat. Serve the shrimp in bowls with a crusty loaf of bread for dipping in the sauce.

Note: Shrimp cook very fast, usually in about 2 minutes. Be careful not to overcook the dish or it will be tough and dry.

Pete's New Orleans Grilled Shrimp with Victoria Taylor's New Orleans Seasoning

PREPARATION TIME: 25 MINUTES
REFRIGERATION TIME: 30 MINUTES TO 2 HOURS / COOKING TIME: 5 MINUTES
SERVES: 6 AS AN APPETIZER

The Shrimp:
1 1/2 pounds shrimp

Marinade:
1/3 cup soy sauce (Tamari brand preferred)
1/2 cup white wine vinegar
3 tablespoons Victoria Taylor's New Orleans Seasoning
1/3 cup toasted sesame oil (regular sesame oil may be used)
3 tablespoons lemon juice
2 tablespoons minced fresh ginger

For the Shrimp: Shell and clean the shrimp, leaving the tails on.

For the Marinade: Combine the soy sauce, vinegar, New Orleans Seasoning, sesame oil, lemon juice and ginger in a bowl and mix well. Add the shrimp to the marinade in a sealable plastic bag. Marinate in the refrigerator for 30 minutes to 2 hours. Prepare the grill for cooking. Grill the shrimp on skewers or on a rack for 2 minutes per side. Place the grilled shrimp in a bowl and encourage people to eat them with their hands, discarding the tails.

Note: This recipe comes from my Godfather, Pete. It's a family favorite. It's one of the reasons that I keep my grill outside all winter.

Main Dishes

Indoor Barbecued Marinated Beef Brisket with Victoria Taylor's Kansas City Seasoning

PREPARATION TIME: 20 MINUTES
REFRIGERATION TIME: OVERNIGHT—TWICE / COOKING TIME: 4^{1}/$_{2}$ HOURS
SERVES: 6 TO 8

    1 beef brisket (6 to 8 pounds), or 2 smaller 3-pound briskets
    ^{1}/$_{4}$ cup Worcestershire sauce
    ^{1}/$_{2}$ cup Victoria Taylor's Kansas City Seasoning
    ^{1}/$_{3}$ cup olive oil
    ^{1}/$_{4}$ cup red wine vinegar
    1 (15-ounce) can tomato sauce
    1 cup KC Masterpiece® BBQ sauce

First Day: Place brisket, fat side up, on a large double sheet of foil in a baking dish. Mix the Worcestershire sauce, Kansas City Seasoning, olive oil, vinegar and tomato sauce in a bowl and pour over the brisket. Seal the foil over the brisket and place in the refrigerator overnight.

Second Day: Preheat the oven to 300 degrees. On the morning of the second day, remove the brisket from the refrigerator and keep covered. Bake for 4 hours. Cool the covered brisket in the refrigerator until 1 hour before serving, overnight if possible. To serve, preheat the oven to 350 degrees. Discard the foil and any excess fat that has formed. Slice the brisket across the grain with a sharp knife. Pour BBQ sauce over the slices and bake for 30 minutes. Serve with additional BBQ sauce, if desired.

Note: This recipe does take 2 days to complete, but the work is minimal. It just takes a little bit of planning—and it's well worth it. Serve with baked beans and coleslaw.

Toasted Onion Pot Roast with Carrots and Potatoes with Victoria Taylor's Toasted Onion Herb Seasoning

PREPARATION TIME: 45 MINUTES / COOKING TIME: 2 HOURS 15 MINUTES
SERVES: 4 TO 6

1 pot roast (2 pounds)
2 tablespoons vegetable oil
1/4 cup flour
1/4 cup Victoria Taylor's Toasted Onion Herb Seasoning
4 carrots, peeled and cut into 1-inch pieces
2 cups red wine (cabernet or red zinfandel)
1 (14-ounce) can beef stock
1 1/2 to 2 pounds new red potatoes
1/2 cup sour cream

Use a Dutch oven or a large saucepan with a cover for this dish. Remove any excess fat from the roast with a sharp knife. Heat the vegetable oil in the pan until hot but not smoking. Coat the roast with the flour to cover it, shaking off any excess. Brown the roast over medium to high heat on all sides. Add the Toasted Onion Herb Seasoning, carrots, wine and stock. Bring to a simmer and cook for 1 1/2 hours, turning the roast over occasionally and adding additional wine, stock or water to the pan as needed to keep at least 1 inch of liquid in the pan. After 1 1/2 hours of cooking, add the potatoes. For small potatoes (1 to 2 inches in diameter), add whole. Cut larger potatoes in half or quarters. Cook the roast with the potatoes for an additional 45 minutes. Remove the roast and the potatoes from the pan to serving plates or bowls and stir the sour cream into the pan juices. Spoon the gravy over the roast and potatoes and serve.

Note: Serve this flavorful winter dish with warm bread. This is the perfect dish to serve with a hearty red wine, such as a cabernet sauvignon or a merlot. Leftover pot roast and potatoes may be stored in the refrigerator and reheated in a saucepan.

Beef Tenderloin with Victoria Taylor's Peppercorn Crust and Parsley Caper Sauce

PREPARATION TIME: 15 MINUTES / COOKING TIME: 45 MINUTES
SERVES: 10 TO 12

The Tenderloin:
1 whole beef tenderloin, trimmed of fat (about 5 pounds)
6 tablespoons Victoria Taylor's Peppermill Mix
2 tablespoons olive oil
1 tablespoon salt (sea salt preferred)

The Sauce:
1/2 cup chopped fresh Italian parsley
1 tablespoon fresh lemon juice
1/4 cup capers, coarsely chopped
3 scallions, finely chopped (white and light green parts only)
1/4 teaspoon salt
1/2 cup extra-virgin olive oil

For the Tenderloin: Bring the tenderloin to room temperature for 1 to 2 hours before cooking. Preheat the oven to 425 degrees. Pat the tenderloin dry and make 3 or 4 small shallow slits in the silver skin of the tenderloin to keep it from curling during roasting. For best results, fold back the thin end of the tenderloin and tie the whole tenderloin with kitchen string every 2 inches. This should even out the thickness of the tenderloin, allowing for even cooking. Crush the Peppermill Mix with a mortar and pestle or use a mallet to crush the peppercorns in a plastic bag until the hard black and white peppercorns begin to break up. Avoid using a food processor or a grinder for crushing the peppers as it will over grind the softer pink and green peppers. Rub the tenderloin with the olive oil and coat with the salt and Peppermill Mix. Place on a rack in a roasting pan. Roast the tenderloin for 45 minutes or until the interior temperature reads 125 degrees. The tenderloin will range from medium to medium-rare. Let the tenderloin stand, loosely covered with foil, for at least 30 minutes before carving.

For the Sauce: Combine the parsley, lemon juice, capers, scallions, salt and olive oil in a bowl and mix well. Serve at room temperature.

Note: To serve the tenderloin, slice it evenly into 1/2-inch slices and arrange on a platter. Serve the sauce on the side and let guests spoon the sauce over the tenderloin to their liking. I always serve tenderloin with a potato dish such as mashed potatoes or roasted potatoes. Round out the meal with a simple green salad.

Onion Herb Beef Roast with Victoria Taylor's Toasted Onion Herb Seasoning

PREPARATION TIME: 10 MINUTES / COOKING TIME: 2¹/2 TO 3 HOURS
SERVES: 8

> olive oil
> 1 beef round roast (3 to 4 pounds)
> 1/4 cup Victoria Taylor's Toasted Onion Herb Seasoning
>   (enough to coat entire roast)
> 1 cup water

Preheat the oven to 350 degrees. Rub olive oil on all sides of roast. Rub Toasted Onion Herb Seasoning all over roast. Place roast on rack in a roasting pan. Add about 1 cup water to the bottom of the roasting pan. Roast for 2¹/2 to 3 hours or until internal temperature reaches 140 degrees. Remove roast from oven, cover with foil and let rest for 15 minutes before carving. Carve the roast into 1/4-inch slices, cutting across the grain.

Note: Carrots, onions, and potatoes may be added to the roasting pan during the last hour of cooking to complete the meal.

Shallot and Cognac Glazed Tenderloin with Victoria Taylor's Peppermill Mix

PREPARATION TIME: 15 MINUTES / COOKING TIME: 45 MINUTES
SERVES: 6

The Tenderloin:
1 whole beef tenderloin, trimmed of fat (about 3 pounds)
3 tablespoons Victoria Taylor's Peppermill Mix
2 tablespoons olive oil
1 tablespoon salt (kosher or sea salt preferred)

The Glaze Sauce:
1 tablespoon butter
1 tablespoon vegetable oil
6 large shallots, minced
1/2 cup cognac
1/2 cup red wine, such as burgundy, pinot noir or merlot

For the Tenderloin: Bring the tenderloin to room temperature for 1 hour before cooking. Preheat the oven to 425 degrees. Pat the tenderloin dry and make 3 or 4 small shallow slits in the silver skin of the tenderloin to keep it from curling during roasting. For best results, fold back the thin end of the tenderloin and tie the whole tenderloin with kitchen string every 2 inches. This should even out the thickness of the tenderloin, allowing for even cooking. Crush the Peppermill Mix with a mortar and pestle or use a mallet to crush the peppercorns in a plastic bag until the hard black and white peppercorns begin to break up. Avoid using a food processor or a grinder for crushing the peppers as it will over grind the softer pink and green peppers. Rub the tenderloin with the olive oil and coat with the salt and Peppermill Mix. Place on a rack in a roasting pan. Roast the tenderloin for 45 minutes or until the interior temperature reads 125 degrees. The tenderloin will range from medium to medium-rare. Let the tenderloin stand, loosely covered with foil, for at least 30 minutes before carving.

For the Sauce: Take the roasting pan with reserved juices and place it over medium heat. Melt the butter and add the vegetable oil to the pan. Add the shallots and cook for 3 to 4 minutes, stirring frequently. Add the cognac to the pan. It's optional to ignite the cognac before proceeding. If ignited, the flame will burn out in about 10 seconds. Add the red wine and simmer until reduced by one-third, about 6 to 8 minutes. Slice the tenderloin into 1-inch pieces and serve, spooning the glaze over the top.

Texas Butter for Steaks with Victoria Taylor's Texas Red Seasoning

PREPARATION TIME: 20 MINUTES
SERVES: 8

1/2 cup (1 stick) butter, softened
2 tablespoons roasted red pepper, finely chopped
2 tablespoons minced shallot
1 teaspoon Victoria Taylor's Texas Red Seasoning
1 teaspoon fresh lemon juice
2 tablespoons chopped fresh parsley
salt and pepper to taste

Place the softened butter in a bowl. Add the roasted red pepper, shallot, Texas Red Seasoning, lemon juice, parsley, salt and pepper and mix well. Spoon butter mixture onto the center of an 8-inch piece of plastic wrap. Shape into an 1 1/2-inch-diameter tube, twisting both ends of plastic wrap to seal. Chill until ready to serve. Cut 1/2-inch slices to use on steak, hot from the grill, allowing it to melt into a sauce.

Note: This incredibly flavorful butter can be used on fish steaks as well as beef steaks. It's also great on vegetables and potatoes.

Grilled Beef Tenderloin and Garlic Feast with Victoria Taylor's Kansas City Seasoning

PREPARATION TIME: 30 MINUTES / COOKING TIME: 45 MINUTES
SERVES: 4

The Roasted Garlic:
4 heads garlic
1/4 cup olive oil

The Garlic Mashed Potatoes:
2 pounds red bliss potatoes
6 cloves garlic, peeled
4 tablespoons butter
3/4 to 1 cup milk
salt and pepper to taste

The Steaks:
4 tenderloin steaks, 1 to 1 1/2 inches thick
1/4 cup olive oil
1/4 cup Victoria Taylor's Kansas City Seasoning
salt and pepper to taste

For the Roasted Garlic: Prepare the grill for cooking with medium to high heat. Slice the tops off each of the heads of garlic to expose the cloves. Place each garlic head on a separate piece of foil and drizzle 1 tablespoon olive oil on each head. Use the foil to make loose pouches around the garlic. Transfer the garlic pouches to the grill rack over medium to high heat and cover the grill. Roast the garlic for 30 to 35 minutes.

For the Garlic Mashed Potatoes: Boil the unpeeled red potatoes with the peeled garlic in enough water to cover in a saucepan for 25 minutes. Drain the potatoes and garlic and return to the pan. Mash the potatoes by hand adding the butter, milk and salt and pepper to taste.

For the Steaks: Rub each steak with 1 tablespoon olive oil and 1 tablespoon Kansas City Seasoning. Grill over medium to high heat for 8 to 10 minutes on the first side and 6 to 8 minutes on the second side for medium-rare. Serve the steaks on a bed of Garlic Mashed Potatoes accompanied by the Roasted Garlic. Complete the feast with a seasonal green vegetable.

Note: Roasted garlic has a completely different character than fresh. While fresh garlic is pungent and savory, roasted garlic is mild and slightly sweet.

Filets Mignons with Mustard Peppercorn Crust with Victoria Taylor's Peppermill Mix

PREPARATION TIME: 10 MINUTES / COOKING TIME: 10 MINUTES
SERVES: 4

3 tablespoons Victoria Taylor's Peppermill Mix
4 steaks, 5 to 8 ounces each (filet mignon or rib-eye)
1/4 cup Dijon mustard

Crush the Peppermill Mix with a mortar and pestle or use a mallet to crush them in a plastic bag until the hard black peppercorns begin to break up. Coat the steaks with the Dijon mustard, then press the crushed pepper into all sides of the steaks. Let the steaks rest while you prepare the grill. Grill over medium to high heat for 4 to 5 minutes per side for medium-rare.

Note: You have probably heard this before: Steaks continue to cook after you remove them from the grill. They *really* do. Remove a steak from the grill when it is rare to medium-rare and you will end up with a medium to medium-rare steak.

Grilled Flank Steak with Victoria Taylor's New Orleans Seasoning

PREPARATION TIME: 10 MINUTES
REFRIGERATION TIME: OVERNIGHT / COOKING TIME: 12 TO 16 MINUTES
SERVES: 4 TO 6

1 1/2 pounds flank steak, trimmed
1 cup prepared barbecue sauce or French dressing
2 tablespoons vinegar
3 tablespoons Victoria Taylor's New Orleans Seasoning
1/2 can cola

Combine the flank steak, barbecue sauce, vinegar, New Orleans Seasoning and cola in a sealable plastic bag and refrigerate overnight. Remove the steak from the marinade and grill over charcoal or in grill pan until done, about 6 to 8 minutes per side. Slice at an angle across the grain into very thin strips. Serve with rice and a vegetable.

Kansas City Grilled Steak with Victoria Taylor's Kansas City Seasoning

PREPARATION TIME: 15 MINUTES / COOKING TIME: 12 MINUTES
SERVES: 4

8 teaspoons Victoria Taylor's Kansas City Seasoning
4 single-serving size steaks, such as fillet, rib-eye, sirloin or T-bone
   (5 to 8 ounces)

Prepare the grill for cooking with medium to high heat. Coat all sides of the steaks with the Kansas City Seasoning and let them rest while you prepare the fire. Use of a charcoal grill is preferred. Start the coals in a pile and spread them when you are ready to cook. Coals for grilling should be in a thick single layer.

Place the steaks on the grill for 5 to 6 minutes per side. This should yield medium to medium-rare results. The steaks will continue to cook for several minutes after they are removed from the grill. Serve with baked or mashed potatoes and a small salad.

Grilled Sirloin and Shallot and Red Pepper Aioli with Victoria Taylor's Kansas City Seasoning

PREPARATION TIME: 20 MINUTES / COOKING TIME: 8 MINUTES
SERVES: 4

The Steak:
2 pounds sirloin steak (3/4 to 1 inch thick)
2 tablespoons olive oil
3 tablespoons Victoria Taylor's Kansas City Seasoning

The Shallot and Red Pepper Aioli:
1/4 cup mayonnaise
1/4 cup roasted sweet red bell pepper
2 medium shallots

For the Steak: Prepare the grill for cooking with medium to high heat. Coat the steak with the olive oil. Now rub the steaks with the Kansas City Seasoning and set aside.

For the Shallot and Red Pepper Aioli: In a food processor, combine the mayonnaise, roasted pepper and shallots. Pulse several times until well mixed. Grill the steaks over medium-high heat for 3 1/2 minutes per side for medium-rare. Slice the steak(s) in long strips and arrange on a platter. Drizzle the Shallot and Red Pepper Aioli over the steak and serve immediately. Serve with a baked potato and a garden salad with a simple vinaigrette.

Texas Red Chili with Victoria Taylor's Texas Red Seasoning

PREPARATION TIME: 30 MINUTES / COOKING TIME: 2 HOURS
SERVES: 6

3 tablespoons peanut oil
1 large onion, chopped
1/4 cup Victoria Taylor's Texas Red Seasoning
   (add more for heat lovers)
1 teaspoon salt
2 pounds beef bottom round, cut into 1/2-inch pieces
3 slices uncooked bacon, finely chopped
1 (28-ounce) can crushed tomatoes
1 3/4 cups beef stock
1 (6-ounce) can tomato paste
2 tablespoons dark brown sugar

Heat the peanut oil in a large stockpot or Dutch oven. Add the onion, Texas Red Seasoning and salt and sauté over medium heat for 3 minutes. Add the beef and bacon and cook over high heat for about 10 to 15 minutes or until the beef is browned, stirring frequently. Add the crushed tomatoes, beef stock, tomato paste and brown sugar. Simmer, uncovered, for 2 hours, stirring occasionally. Add more stock if the chili gets too thick and starts to stick to the pot. After 2 hours, the chili may be covered and kept warm on low heat.

Note: This is the real thing, real beef and no beans. So it's very rich and filling. I think the condiments are key for this dish to lighten it up and add color. Serve with bowls of finely diced red onion, finely diced yellow and red bell peppers, grated cheese, and a large bowl of corn chips.

Sunday Supper Chili for a Crowd with Victoria Taylor's Texas Red Seasoning

PREPARATION: 30 MINUTES / COOKING TIME: 2 HOURS
SERVES: 8

2 large onions, chopped
2½ pounds ground beef
1½ teaspoons salt
¼ cup Victoria Taylor's Texas Red Seasoning
    (add more for heat lovers)
1 large green bell pepper, cut into ¼-inch pieces
3 stalks celery, cut into ¼-inch pieces
1 (28-ounce) can crushed tomatoes
1 (28-ounce) can diced tomatoes
2 cups water
2 (15- to 19-ounce) cans kidney beans, drained
sour cream
grated Cheddar cheese
chopped red onion

Sauté the onions and ground beef in a large pot over medium-high heat for 10 minutes or until the ground beef is just cooked. Stir in the salt and the Texas Red Seasoning. Add the green pepper, celery, crushed tomatoes, diced tomatoes and water. Cook, covered, on a low boil for 1 hour. Remove the cover and cook for 45 minutes, stirring occasionally. Add the beans and cook for an additional 15 minutes. Serve with bowls of sour cream, grated cheese and chopped red onion, if desired. This chili freezes well. Just thaw and heat through before serving.

Note: The recommended ¼ cup Texas Red Seasoning in this recipe gives a mild heat. I use ½ cup when I make it because I prefer a fairly spicy-hot chili.

Spaghetti Pie with Victoria Taylor's Sicilian Seasoning

PREPARATION TIME: 30 MINUTES / COOKING TIME: 1 HOUR
SERVES: 10 TO 12

First Layer:

2 pounds spaghetti
2 tablespoons sea salt

Second Layer:

16 ounces cottage cheese
16 ounces cream cheese
16 ounces sour cream
16 ounces ricotta cheese

Third Layer:

2 large onions, chopped
2 tablespoons olive oil
2 tablespoons butter
2½ pounds ground beef
¼ cup Victoria Taylor's Sicilian Seasoning
1 (28-ounce) can crushed tomatoes
1 (15-ounce) can tomato sauce
1 (6-ounce) can tomato paste

For the Third Layer: Start preparing the third layer first because it takes the longest. Sauté the chopped onions in the olive oil in a large skillet over medium-high heat for 5 minutes or until tender. Add the butter. Add the ground beef and cook until browned and crumbly, stirring frequently. Add the Sicilian Seasoning, crushed tomatoes, tomato sauce and tomato paste and mix well. Keep this mixture on a low simmer while you prepare the spaghetti and the cheese layer of the pie.

For the First Layer: Bring enough water to cover 2 pounds of pasta to a boil in a stockpot. Add the spaghetti and sea salt to the water and cook using the package directions.

For the Second Layer: Combine the cottage cheese, cream cheese, sour cream and ricotta cheese in a large bowl and mix well. As soon as the pasta is cooked and drained, you are ready to assemble the pie.

Use one very large lasagna pan (3- to 4-inch sides) or 2 medium-size Pyrex pans (9x13-inch) for this dish. If you use one large pan, your layers will be a little thicker. The finished pie has a total of 6 layers: 1) spaghetti, 2) cheese, 3) meat sauce, 4) spaghetti, 5) cheese 6) meat sauce. Preheat the oven to 350 degrees. Layer 1/2 of the spaghetti on the bottom of the pan(s). Spread 1/2 of the cheese mixture over the spaghetti using a spatula. Now spread a little less than 1/2 of the meat sauce over the cheese. Repeat these 3 steps, finishing with a generous layer of remaining meat sauce. Bake the pie for 1 hour. Let the pie rest for 5 minutes before serving. The pie may be frozen for up to 2 months. For frozen spaghetti pie, simply thaw and cook as above.

Note: This is a big recipe. But if you are going to make it, go for it. Use 3 smaller casseroles and freeze the pies you don't need for later. The world seems a little brighter when you know you have a reserve of spaghetti pie in the freezer.

Texas Soft Tacos with Victoria Taylor's Texas Red Seasoning

PREPARATION TIME: 10 MINUTES / COOKING TIME: 10 MINUTES
SERVES: 4

    1 pound ground beef
    2 tablespoons Victoria Taylor's Texas Red Seasoning
    1 packet of tortillas
    tomato, lettuce, shredded cheese, sour cream, salsa
      (optional for garnish)

Combine the ground beef and Texas Red Seasoning in a skillet. Cook until the ground beef is browned and crumbly, about 10 minutes. Drain off excess fat. Place on tortilla with any combination of garnish that you like. Serve with red beans and rice (or place the red beans and rice in the tortilla as well).

Note: If you are a fan of spicy food, add an extra tablespoon of Texas Red Seasoning to this recipe.

Easy Classic Meat Loaf with Victoria Taylor's Toasted Onion Herb Seasoning

PREPARATION TIME: 10 MINUTES / COOKING TIME: 50 MINUTES
SERVES: 4

1 pound ground beef
1/4 cup ketchup
1 tablespoon prepared mustard
1/2 cup plain bread crumbs
1 egg
2 tablespoons Victoria Taylor's Toasted Onion Herb Seasoning

Preheat the oven to 350 degrees. Combine the ground beef, ketchup, mustard, bread crumbs, egg and Toasted Onion Herb Seasoning in a bowl and mix well. Shape into a round loaf. Place in a baking pan or dish. Bake for 50 minutes. Remove from oven and let rest for 5 minutes before serving.

Note: A plain old baked potato is always good with meat loaf. I allow an hour for baked potatoes at 350 degrees, so I usually put them in the oven a few minutes before the meat loaf.

Toasted Onion Herb Burgers with Victoria Taylor's Toasted Onion Herb Seasoning

PREPARATION TIME: 10 MINUTES / COOKING TIME: 10 TO 12 MINUTES
SERVES: 4

    1 pound lean ground beef
    3 tablespoons Victoria Taylor's Toasted Onion Herb Seasoning
    2 tablespoons unseasoned dry bread crumbs
    2 teaspoons prepared mustard
    sliced cheese (optional)

Preheat the grill for cooking. Combine the ground beef, Toasted Onion Herb Seasoning, bread crumbs and mustard in a bowl and mix well. Shape into 4 patties. Cook on charcoal grill, gas grill or heavy skillet for 6 to 8 minutes or until juice beads up on the top side of burgers. Flip over and top with cheese. Cook for an additional 4 minutes or until desired degree of doneness.

Note: Ask any famous chef what his/her favorite dish is, and three out of four will say a great cheeseburger. I'm not surprised.

Easy Egg Noodle Feast with Victoria Taylor's Toasted Onion Herb Seasoning

PREPARATION TIME: 10 MINUTES / COOKING TIME: 10 MINUTES
SERVES: 2 TO 4

    1 pound ground beef
    2 tablespoons Victoria Taylor's Toasted Onion Herb Seasoning
    1/2 cup sour cream
    1 package egg noodles

Combine the ground beef and Toasted Onion Herb Seasoning in a skillet. Cook until ground beef is browned and crumbly, about 10 minutes. Drain off excess fat. Mix in sour cream. Cook the egg noodles using the package directions. Serve the ground beef mixture over the egg noodles.

Note: Add sautéed mushrooms to this dish. The mushrooms may be added to the browned ground beef and sautéed for 5 minutes or just until tender.

Stuffed Peppers and Tomatoes with Victoria Taylor's Mediterranean Seasoning

PREPARATION TIME: 30 MINUTES / COOKING TIME: 1 HOUR
SERVES: 4

2 medium onions, finely chopped
4 cloves garlic, minced
$^1/_3$ cup pure or light olive oil, divided
1 pound ground beef
1 (14-ounce) can diced or crushed tomatoes
1 small zucchini, finely chopped
$^1/_4$ cup pine nuts
$^3/_4$ cup regular long grain white rice (uncooked)
3 tablespoons Victoria Taylor's Mediterranean Seasoning
8 large peppers or tomatoes or any combination

Sauté the onions and garlic in 2 tablespoons of the olive oil in a large skillet for 3 minutes. Add the ground beef and cook until browned and crumbly. Add the diced tomatoes, zucchini, pine nuts, rice and Mediterranean Seasoning. Stir briefly and remove from the heat. Prepare the peppers and/or tomatoes for stuffing: Slice the tops ($^1/_2$-inch "lids") off the peppers and/or tomatoes and set them aside. Hollow out the peppers and/or tomatoes, discarding the scooped out material. Preheat the oven to 375 degrees. Place the peppers and/or tomatoes in a roasting pan just large enough to hold them and fill them with the stuffing. Drizzle $^1/_2$ of the remaining olive oil on the stuffed peppers and/or tomatoes and replace their tops or "lids." Drizzle with the last of the olive oil. Bake for 1 hour to 1$^1/_4$ hours. Serve with sliced bread and feta cheese.

Note: In the summer, when the colorful bell peppers are in season (and less expensive), it's fun to use a combination of green, yellow, red and orange bell peppers in this dish. I usually make 4 peppers and 4 tomatoes, so each person gets one of each.

Corn Bread-Stuffed Pork Chops with Victoria Taylor's New Orleans Seasoning

PREPARATION TIME: 15 MINUTES / COOKING TIME: 35 MINUTES
SERVES: 4

The Stuffing:
1/4 cup chopped onion (1/2 medium onion)
1 clove garlic, minced
1 tablespoon butter
1/2 cup corn bread stuffing mix
1/4 cup chopped seeded tomato
1/2 (4-ounce) can chopped green chiles, drained
1 tablespoon Victoria Taylor's New Orleans Seasoning

The Pork Chops:
4 pork loin rib chops, cut 1 1/4 inches thick
red jalapeño jelly (optional)

For the Stuffing: Cook the onion and garlic in hot butter in a small saucepan until tender, stirring constantly. Stir in the stuffing mix, tomato, green chiles and New Orleans Seasoning.

For the Pork Chops: Preheat the oven to 375 degrees. Trim fat from chops. Cut a pocket in each chop by cutting from fat side almost to bone or about 1/4 inch from bottom for boneless chops. Place about 1/4 cup of stuffing in each chop. Arrange chops on a rack in a shallow roasting pan. Bake for 35 to 45 minutes or until no pink remains and juices run clear. Meanwhile, if desired, cook jalapeño jelly in a small saucepan until heated through. Brush over chops before the last 5 minutes of baking.

Note: If necessary, secure pork chops with wooden picks. Serve with rice or mashed potatoes and a vegetable.

Pork au Poivre with Victoria Taylor's Peppermill Mix

PREPARATION: 30 MINUTES / COOKING TIME: 30 MINUTES
SERVES: 4

2 tablespoons Victoria Taylor's Peppermill Mix
4 pork or veal chops (6 to 8 ounces each)
olive oil
4 ounces mushrooms, sliced
1 small yellow onion, sliced thinly
1 shallot, minced
1 tablespoon flour
2 tablespoons sherry
1/2 cup beef stock
1/2 cup white wine
1 tablespoon brown sugar
salt to taste
2 tablespoons sour cream or heavy cream

Preheat the oven to 375 degrees. Crush 2 tablespoons Peppermill Mix with a peppermill or mortar and pestle or use a mallet to crush the peppercorns in a bag. Crush the pepper until the hard black and white peppercorns begin to break up. Press the crushed pepper into all sides of the chops. Heat olive oil in heavy, ovenproof skillet and cook mushrooms, onion and shallot in the hot oil until tender, about 10 minutes. Remove from skillet and set aside in a small bowl. Turn heat up to high. Add additional olive oil if needed and sear chops on both sides, keeping warm on plate tented with foil until all chops are seared. Turn off heat. Return all chops and any residual juices and the mushroom mixture to the skillet. Bake for 15 minutes or until firm to the touch. Keep the cooked chops warm on a clean, foil-tented plate, and drain all but 1 teaspoon of drippings from skillet. Place skillet over medium heat. Add flour to the skillet drippings to make a sauce. Cook for 2 minutes, stirring constantly to avoid burning. Add sherry gradually to the skillet and stir to incorporate. Add beef stock, white wine and brown sugar.

Boil for 8 minutes or until the sauce reduces to a syrupy consistency. Adjust the sauce with salt to taste, if needed. Remove from heat. Stir in sour cream. Serve sauce spooned over pork chops. Serve with baked or mashed potatoes and some steamed or sautéed broccoli.

Note: If you love pork and pepper, you must try this recipe. The flavor is amazing, and the recipe is much easier than it looks.

Cheddar Cheese and Ham Frittata with Victoria Taylor's Holiday Seasoning

PREPARATION TIME: 10 MINUTES / COOKING TIME: 10 MINUTES
SERVES: 2

    3 scallions, chopped
    2 tablespoons olive oil
    6 eggs
    2 tablespoons Victoria Taylor's Holiday Seasoning
    1 (6-ounce) ham steak, cubed
    1/2 cup grated Cheddar cheese

Preheat the broiler to high. Cook the scallions in the olive oil in a medium ovenproof skillet until tender, about 3 minutes. Whisk eggs and Holiday Seasoning in a bowl. Add egg mixture to scallions and cook without stirring for about 2 minutes. Add the ham and cook until hot and edges of frittata are set (center should still be soft). Sprinkle Cheddar cheese on frittata and broil until cheese is bubbly, about 1 to 2 minutes. Serve cut into wedges with fresh fruit.

Note: This easy recipe may be modified by substituting tomatoes or sausage for the ham.

Texas Chops with Victoria Taylor's Texas Red Seasoning

PREPARATION TIME: 5 MINUTES / COOKING TIME: 15 MINUTES
SERVES: 4

    4 center-cut, bone-in pork chops
    2 teaspoons Victoria Taylor's Texas Red Seasoning
    1 to 2 tablespoons peanut oil
    fresh lime

Rinse pork chops and pat dry. Sprinkle each side of the chops with
1/4 teaspoon Texas Red Seasoning, patting lightly. Heat peanut oil in
heavy skillet, cast-iron if available, over medium heat. Arrange chops in
skillet and cook for 8 to 12 minutes on first side, depending on thickness.
Flip over and cook for 5 to 7 minutes. Serve with a squeeze of fresh
lime atop white rice. Goes well with corn on the cob or fresh sliced
cucumbers with oil and vinegar.

Note: This mixture is hot and may emit spicy smoke from the pan. Keep
well ventilated or grill outside on an oiled rack.

KC BBQ Pork Roast with Victoria Taylor's Kansas City Seasoning

PREPARATION TIME: 10 MINUTES / COOKING TIME: 2 TO 3 HOURS
SERVES: 6

1 boneless pork roast (3 pounds)
3 tablespoons Victoria Taylor's Kansas City Seasoning

Coat the roast with the Kansas City Seasoning and let it stand while you prepare the fire. Use of a charcoal grill is preferred. Stack a medium to large mound of coals on one side of the grill and start the fire. You will be cooking on the other side, away from the coals. Barbecuing, in contrast to grilling, requires indirect heat for slow cooking. Put about 4 cups of wood chips (hickory or mesquite are fine) in a bucket with water. If possible, soak your wood chips several hours ahead. This makes for better smoke. Place the roast as far away from the hot coals as possible. Every half hour or so, throw some wet wood chips on the coals. Keep the grill covered at all times with the vents open. Barbecue the roast for 2 to 3 hours. Smaller roasts will take less time.

Note: When you are making BBQ (in contrast to grilling), you will see a thin pink line on the outside layer of the pork. This is from the smoke during cooking. Barbecue pros look for a nice pink line.

Stuffed Tuscan Pork Loin Roast with Victoria Taylor's Tuscan Seasoning

PREPARATION TIME: 30 MINUTES / COOKING TIME: 1^1/$_2$ HOURS
SERVES: 4 TO 6

1 to 2 pounds boneless pork loin, trimmed of fat
1 shallot, minced
^{1}/$_3$ pound cremini or button mushrooms, sliced thinly
1 tablespoon olive oil or butter
1 tablespoon brandy or sherry
3 tablespoons Victoria Taylor's Tuscan Seasoning, divided
salt and pepper to taste
2 ounces goat cheese or cream cheese
2 ounces roasted red peppers, chopped
unseasoned dry bread crumbs (enough to coat roast)

Preheat the oven to 325 degrees. Trim the loin of any visible fat. Using a sharp knife, cut the loin as if you were unrolling a jelly roll. Using the knife carefully, unroll the loin to achieve a ^{1}/$_2$-inch-flat loin. Pound the unrolled flat loin to ensure an even thickness throughout. In a sauté pan over medium heat, cook the shallot and mushrooms in olive oil or butter until they soften, about 6 to 8 minutes. Let stand to cool. Rub the pork on the top side with the brandy and sprinkle 2 tablespoons of the Tuscan Seasoning evenly across the top. Season the loin with salt and pepper to taste. Distribute the goat cheese, cooked mushroom mixture and red peppers along the length of the loin, in a thin strip, about 2 inches from one side. Roll the loin back up starting with the side containing the stuffing, and fasten together with wooden picks or truss with kitchen string, trying also to pinch together the ends. Combine the bread crumbs with the remaining Tuscan Seasoning. Coat the outside of the rolled loin with additional olive oil and pat with seasoned bread crumbs. Place the rolled loin on rack in roasting pan. Bake, uncovered, for 1^1/$_2$ hours or until the internal temperature reaches 155 degrees. Remove from oven and let rest for 10 minutes before cutting into ^{1}/$_2$-inch slices. Serve with oven-roasted potatoes and a seasonal green vegetable.

Pulled Pork Sandwich for the Slow Cooker with Victoria Taylor's Kansas City Seasoning

PREPARATION TIME: 10 MINUTES / COOKING TIME: 6^1/$_2$ TO 11 HOURS
SERVES: 6 TO 8

1 (3-pound) pork roast
7 to 8 tablespoons Victoria Taylor's Kansas City Seasoning
^{1}/$_2$ cup red wine vinegar
2 teaspoons brown sugar
1 onion
1 (19-ounce) bottle KC Masterpiece BBQ Sauce
salt and pepper to taste
coleslaw and dill pickle slices (optional)

Completely coat the roast with the Kansas City Seasoning. Add the vinegar and brown sugar to the bottom of the slow cooker and mix together. Cut the onion in half and place flat on the bottom of the slow cooker. Place the roast on top of the onion; cover. Cook on high for 6 hours or on low for 10 hours. Drain some of the excess juices from the slow cooker. Take two forks and shred or pull the pork from the roast. Add the BBQ Sauce and cook for 30 minutes on high or 1 hour on low. Serve on a bulkie roll. For extra taste, layer the pulled pork with coleslaw and dill pickle slices on the roll.

Note: Set up your slow cooker to cook in the morning and by afternoon your kitchen (and house) will be filled with the incredibly mouthwatering aroma of this recipe. There will not be any left over.

Curried Pork Satay with Victoria Taylor's Curry

PREPARATION TIME: 15 MINUTES
REFRIGERATION TIME: 2 HOURS / COOKING TIME: 15 MINUTES
SERVES: 4

1 pork tenderloin (1½ pounds)
2 tablespoons Victoria Taylor's Curry
6 tablespoons orange juice
¼ cup coconut milk
1 teaspoon dark soy sauce
1 tablespoon minced gingerroot
2 teaspoons sesame oil

Trim pork tenderloin of all visible fat and silver skin, the tough stringy membrane usually found at the thick end. Cut pork into 1-inch cubes. Mix the Curry, orange juice, coconut milk, soy sauce, gingerroot and sesame oil in a bowl. Add pork cubes. Marinate in the refrigerator for at least 2 hours. Preheat the grill for cooking or broiler. If using wooden skewers, soak in water for 30 minutes to avoid burning, then thread cubes down to 3 inches from the bottom. Cook on grill or under broiler for 12 to 15 minutes or until pork is firm to the touch and just past pink on the inside, turning frequently. Serve as an appetizer or as a main course over basmati or jasmine rice, along with summer squash and sliced mango.

Note: This recipe calls for 2 hours of marinating time, but you can marinate longer, if desired. Marinate overnight if possible for an even tastier flavor.

KC BBQ Pork Ribs with Victoria Taylor's Kansas City Seasoning

PREPARATION TIME: 10 MINUTES / COOKING TIME: 3 TO 4 HOURS
SERVES: 2

> 1 full slab pork ribs, St. Louis cut preferred
> 3 to 4 tablespoons Victoria Taylor's Kansas City Seasoning

Coat the ribs with the Kansas City Seasoning and let them stand while you prepare the fire. Use of a charcoal grill is preferred. Stack a medium to large mound of coals on one side of the grill and start the fire. You will be cooking on the other side, away from the coals. Barbecuing, in contrast to grilling, requires indirect heat for slow cooking. Put about 4 cups of wood chips (hickory or mesquite are fine) in a bucket with water. If possible, soak your wood chips several hours ahead. This makes for better smoke, but I usually forget. Place the ribs as far away from the hot coals as possible. You may need to cut the slabs in half or stack the ribs. This is fine as you can rotate them during cooking. Every half hour or so, throw some wet wood chips on the coals. Keep the grill covered at all times with the vents open. Barbecue the ribs for 3 to 4 hours, moving them periodically as needed. For accompaniments, serve coleslaw and corn bread or baked beans.

Note: You will know your ribs are just right if the pork is close to falling off the bone. I only use barbecue sauce as a condiment on the table. Most of them are tomato based and will burn as soon as they are exposed to direct heat on a grill.

Veal Saltimbocca with Victoria Taylor's Holiday Seasoning

PREPARATION TIME: 20 MINUTES / COOKING TIME: 10 MINUTES
SERVES: 4

2 tablespoons olive oil
veal cutlets (about 1½ pounds)
2 tablespoons Victoria Taylor's Holiday Seasoning
flour for dredging
1 cup sweet sherry or marsala
8 to 12 thin slices prosciutto (1 per veal slice)
³/₄ cup shredded mozzarella or fontina cheese
1 tablespoon butter
salt and pepper to taste
1 lemon (optional for garnish)

Heat the olive oil until hot but not smoking in a large heavy skillet. Sprinkle veal cutlets with Holiday Seasoning and coat with flour, shaking off excess. Cook in batches for 2 minutes per side and transfer to a plate, covering loosely with aluminum foil to keep warm. Add sherry or wine to skillet to deglaze, scraping up browned bits from pan. Boil until liquid is reduced by one-third. Add veal and any juices back to skillet and top with a slice of prosciutto, working again in batches. Sprinkle shredded cheese evenly over each piece. Cover and cook for 1 to 2 minutes to warm prosciutto and melt cheese. Remove to dinner plates. Swirl butter into sauce before pouring evenly over each serving. Season with salt and pepper to taste. Squeeze lemon over each as a final garnish.

Note: The key with any veal preparation is not to overcook the veal. Cook just until done, then remove from heat and continue with the recipe.

Veal Medallions with Maple Dijon Sauce with Victoria Taylor's Herbes de Provence

PREPARATION TIME: 15 MINUTES / COOKING TIME: 20 MINUTES
SERVES: 4

  flour for dredging
  salt and pepper to taste
  2 tablespoons olive oil
  1 1/2 pounds pounded veal cutlets
  1 large white onion, halved and sliced
  1 cup white wine
  1 tablespoon Victoria Taylor's Herbes de Provence
  1/4 cup good quality Dijon mustard
  3 tablespoons maple syrup
  sour cream (optional for garnish)

Combine flour, salt and pepper on a plate and mix well. Heat olive oil in a deep skillet until hot but not smoking. Lightly coat veal cutlets with flour mixture. Cook until browned, about 2 to 3 minutes per side, working in batches to avoid crowding. Remove browned veal to plate and cover loosely with foil to keep warm. Add onion and sauté over low to medium heat until limp, about 6 to 8 minutes. Add wine gradually, stirring to release browned bits off the bottom of the skillet. Bring to a boil. Reduce heat to low. Add Herbes de Provence, Dijon mustard and maple syrup, stirring well to blend. Simmer for 15 minutes. Add veal back to skillet with any residual juices and cook until veal is heated through. Serve with buttered bow tie pasta and garnish with a dollop of sour cream.

Note: Be sure to time the veal during cooking, and remove from heat when first cooked. Veal should be tender and juicy. Overcooked veal can be tough and chewy.

Veal Piccata with Victoria Taylor's Herbes de Provence

PREPARATION TIME: 10 MINUTES / COOKING TIME: 10 MINUTES
SERVES: 4

3 lemons
1/2 cup flour
3 tablespoons Victoria Taylor's Herbes de Provence
11/2 to 2 pounds veal cutlets
2 tablespoons olive oil
2 tablespoons butter
1/4 cup dry white wine
2 tablespoons capers

Juice 2 of the lemons and set aside the juice. Cut off the ends of the third lemon and cut lemon in half lengthwise. Remove the seeds and slice the lemon halves thinly (1/8-inch slices) and set aside. Combine the flour with the Herbes de Provence in a shallow bowl. Coat the cutlets with the flour mixture. Heat the olive oil and butter in a large sauté pan until hot but not smoking. Sauté the cutlets just until cooked, about 2 to 3 minutes per side. Place the cooked cutlets on a plate and cover with foil to keep warm. Now add the lemon juice, lemon slices, white wine and capers to the sauté pan and cook for about 3 minutes on medium to high heat to reduce the sauce. Return the cutlets to the pan and cook for 1 minute longer. Serve the cutlets with the sautéed lemon slices and caper sauce.

Note: This is an amazingly flavorful recipe. The juice and flavor from 3 whole lemons makes this dish a little tangy and delicious.

Veal Birds with Victoria Taylor's Herbes de Provence

PREPARATION TIME: 30 MINUTES / COOKING TIME: 1 HOUR
SERVES: 4

1/2 cup dried currants
2/3 cup port
1 1/2 pounds veal cutlets
1/2 cup flour
3 tablespoons Victoria Taylor's Herbes de Provence
1 pound bacon
2 1/2 tablespoons cornstarch
2 1/2 cups warm water

Combine the currants and port in a small bowl. To prepare the birds, cut the veal cutlets into long strips about 1 1/2 inches wide. Combine 1/2 cup flour and Herbes de Provence on a plate. Coat the veal strips with the flour mixture. Place about 6 to 8 port-soaked currants on one end of the strip. Reserve any remaining currants and the port for later. Roll up the veal strip and wrap with a piece of bacon, securing with a wooden pick. When securing each bird, pass the wooden pick through the bacon and the veal to keep them tightly rolled. Cook the birds over medium heat in a large skillet, turning occasionally until all sides are well browned, about 20 to 25 minutes. Place cooked birds in a Pyrex baking dish just large enough to hold them. Add the cornstarch to the skillet and combine with the fat from the bacon, scraping any browned bits from the sides and bottom of the pan. Now on medium-low heat, add the water 1/2 cup at a time until well combined. Finally add the remaining port and any leftover currants to the sauce. Cook for 5 to 10 minutes or just until the sauce thickens. Pour the sauce over the birds in the Pyrex dish. Preheat the oven to 350 degrees. Bake for 45 minutes. Serve with wild rice.

Note: I always serve veal birds with wild rice on the side. Add a spoonful of additional sauce on the rice for added flavor.

Grilled Tuscan Veal Chops with Apple Ragout with Victoria Taylor's Tuscan Seasoning

PREPARATION: 30 MINUTES / COOKING TIME: 20 MINUTES
SERVES: 4

    1 cup cold water
    4 medium red apples
    1 medium onion, chopped
    2 tablespoons minced shallots
    4 tablespoons butter
    2 tablespoons applejack, brandy or bourbon
    1 tablespoon honey
    pinch of cinnamon
    4 teaspoons lemon juice
    2 teaspoons Dijon mustard
    salt to taste
    4 bone-in veal or pork chops
    olive oil
    4 teaspoons Victoria Taylor's Tuscan Seasoning

Combine the water, apples, onion and shallots in a saucepan. Bring to boil. Reduce heat to low. Cover and simmer for about 10 minutes; uncover. Add butter, applejack, honey, cinnamon and lemon juice and mix well. Simmer for 10 minutes longer. Stir in mustard and salt to taste. Cover and keep warm on a low simmer. Prepare the grill for cooking with medium to high heat. Rinse veal and pat dry. Coat one side of chops with olive oil and sprinkle with 1/2 teaspoon Tuscan Seasoning, rubbing it gently. Repeat on other side. Grill on oiled rack until cooked to desired doneness, about 6 minutes per side. Transfer from grill to plate. Cover loosely with aluminum foil and let stand for 5 minutes to allow the juices to settle. Stir any juice that collects on the plate into the apples, and serve chops with the apple ragout.

Note: The veal chops can be prepared on the grill and served without the apple ragout, if desired. Simply serve with warm applesauce or baked apples.

Osso Buco with Victoria Taylor's Mediterranean Seasoning

PREPARATION TIME: 1 HOUR / COOKING TIME: 2 HOURS
SERVES: 4

1/2 cup flour
1 teaspoon salt
4 pieces veal shank, cut about 1 1/2 inches thick
2 tablespoons olive oil
2 tablespoons butter
1 cup dry white wine
3 carrots, peeled, cut in half lengthwise and sliced into 1/2-inch pieces
1 medium onion, chopped
1 red bell pepper, cut into 1/4-inch strips
2 tablespoons Victoria Taylor's Mediterranean Seasoning
1 (28-ounce) can diced tomatoes
3 tablespoons fresh lemon juice
2 tablespoons finely chopped lemon peel with none of the white pith
1/4 cup chopped fresh Italian parsley (optional for garnish)

For this dish, choose a high-sided, covered sauté pan that will accommodate all the veal shanks snugly in a single layer without overlapping. Combine the flour and salt in a bowl and mix well. Coat the veal shanks with the flour mixture, shaking off any excess. Heat the olive oil and butter in the pan until hot but not smoking. Brown the veal shanks on both sides over medium to high heat and set them aside. Now add the white wine to the pan and cook over medium heat for about 5 minutes, scraping up any of the brown bits from the bottom. Return the veal shanks to the pan. Add the carrots, onion, bell pepper and Mediterranean Seasoning. Now add the tomatoes, lemon juice and lemon peel. Bring the mixture to a boil and reduce to a simmer; cover. Cook the veal shanks for 2 hours or until the veal falls easily from the bone. Add more white wine or water as needed during the cooking process. When you are ready to serve, garnish the osso buco with the chopped parsley.

Moroccan Lamb Stew with Victoria Taylor's Moroccan Seasoning

PREPARATION TIME: 30 MINUTES / COOKING TIME: 1³/₄ HOURS
SERVES: 4

2 tablespoons light olive oil
1 pound well-trimmed boneless lamb shoulder, cut into 1-inch pieces
1 medium onion, cut into 1-inch pieces
1 teaspoon salt
4 teaspoons Victoria Taylor's Moroccan Seasoning
2 large Yukon gold potatoes, peeled and cut into 1-inch pieces
2 large carrots, peeled and cut into ¹/₂-inch slices
1 medium red bell pepper, cut into ¹/₂-inch strips
¹/₂ cup red wine (red zinfandel or cabernet)
3 small roma or plum tomatoes, cut into 1-inch pieces
2 small zucchini, cut into halves and then quartered into strips

Preheat the oven to 350 degrees. Use a large ovenproof saucepan or casserole dish with a cover or a Dutch oven for this dish. Heat the olive oil in the pan and brown the lamb on all sides. Add the onion, salt and Moroccan Seasoning and continue to cook for 5 minutes. Add the potatoes, carrots and red pepper. Pour the wine over the mixture and stir. Push the lamb underneath the veggies and cover. Bake for 1¹/₂ hours, stirring occasionally. Then add the tomatoes and zucchini. Bake for 15 minutes longer and serve.

Note: This is a hearty stew with a great flavor. It can easily be doubled or tripled for larger groups. Once made, it can be refrigerated or frozen. Just reheat it to serve. I serve this with hot crusty French or Italian bread for dipping.

Curried Roast Leg of Lamb with Victoria Taylor's Curry

PREPARATION TIME: 15 MINUTES / REFRIGERATION TIME: 1 HOUR TO OVERNIGHT
COOKING TIME: ABOUT 2 HOURS
SERVES: 4 TO 6

1/4 cup Victoria Taylor's Curry
2 tablespoons vermouth or sherry
1/4 cup orange juice
1 teaspoon balsamic vinegar
1 teaspoon soy sauce
1 (2- to 3-pound) boneless leg of lamb
1 tablespoon honey
salt and pepper to taste

Prepare marinade by mixing together Curry, vermouth, orange juice, vinegar and soy sauce in a bowl. Trim lamb of all visible fat and add to bowl, marinating in the refrigerator for at least an hour, and overnight if possible. Preheat the oven to 450 degrees. Place lamb on rack in roasting pan, reserving marinade. Roast for 20 minutes and turn oven down to 300 degrees. Roast for 1 hour. Pour and brush half the marinade over the lamb and roast for an additional 20 minutes. Mix the honey into remaining marinade and brush on lamb. Roast for 10 minutes and check to see that internal temperature has reached 140 degrees. Remove from oven and let stand loosely covered by aluminum foil for 10 to 15 minutes, then carve. Season with salt and pepper to taste. Serve with couscous and green beans or another green vegetable.

Note: The honey is added during the last 10 minutes of the cooking time to avoid burning the sugar in the honey. Always add sugar-based ingredients toward the end of roasting for a nice glaze and no burning.

Roasted Moroccan Lamb Chops with Victoria Taylor's Moroccan Seasoning

PREPARATION TIME: 5 MINUTES / COOKING TIME: 25 MINUTES
SERVES: 4

    2 tablespoons (or more) Victoria Taylor's Moroccan Seasoning
    4 (8-ounce) lamb chops

Preheat the oven to 350 degrees. Rub the Moroccan Seasoning over the chops. Arrange on a foil-covered roasting pan. Roast for 25 minutes, turning after 15 minutes. Serve immediately.

Note: Lamb cooks quickly. Don't hesitate to remove the lamb from the oven a little early if you prefer it medium-rare.

Fall Holiday Favorites

Vegetable Medley Roasted Turkey with Victoria Taylor's Holiday Seasoning

Preparation time: 20 minutes / Cooking time: 3¹/₂ to 5¹/₂ hours
Serves: 6 to 8

    1 family-size turkey (15 to 22 pounds)
    3 tablespoons olive oil, divided
    4 to 5 tablespoons Victoria Taylor's Holiday Seasoning, divided
    2 large carrots, cut into 1-inch pieces
    1 large onion, cut into 1-inch pieces
    3 cloves garlic, chopped
    1 cup leafy celery tops, cut into 1-inch pieces

To prepare the turkey, remove the giblets and neck. If you plan on making your own gravy, place the giblets and neck in 5 cups water and bring to a boil. Simmer for 1 hour to make turkey stock. Strain the stock and set it aside for gravy and basting the turkey. Preheat the oven to 325 degrees. Rinse the turkey with cool water and pat dry. In a sealable plastic bag, combine 2 tablespoons of the olive oil, 2 tablespoons of the Holiday Seasoning, carrots, onion, garlic and celery and shake to mix well. Stuff the turkey neck and main cavity with the vegetable mixture. Don't bother sewing the cavities up. Leaving them open will add to the juices and flavor. Use the remaining olive oil to coat the turkey breast and legs. Working with your hands to loosen the skin from the turkey breast, spread remaining Holiday Seasoning between the turkey skin and the turkey breast. Place the turkey on a rack in a roasting pan. Roast for 15 minutes per pound, basting with pan juices every 45 minutes. Remove the turkey from the pan, place on the cutting surface and cover tightly with foil. Let rest for 20 minutes before carving. Leave the vegetable mixture in the turkey. This stuffing is to flavor the turkey not to eat.

Note: The keys to this juicy and flavorful turkey are the Holiday Seasoning and the additional flavor and cooking juices provided by the vegetable medley "stuffing." Stuffing the turkey with a portion of the meal's bread-based stuffing just makes the stuffing wet and the turkey dry.

Lemon and Garlic Roasted Turkey with Victoria Taylor's Holiday Seasoning

PREPARATION TIME: 20 MINUTES / COOKING TIME: 3½ TO 5½ HOURS
SERVES: 6 TO 8

    1 family-size turkey (15 to 22 pounds)
    3 tablespoons olive oil, divided
    4 to 5 tablespoons Victoria Taylor's Holiday Seasoning, divided
    2 lemons, quartered
    1 orange, cut into 1-inch pieces
    8 garlic cloves, cut in half
    1 cup leafy celery tops, cut into 1-inch pieces

To prepare the turkey, remove the giblets and neck. If you plan to make your own gravy, place the giblets and neck in 5 cups water and bring to a boil. Simmer for 1 hour to make turkey stock. Strain the stock and set it aside until it's time to make the gravy. Preheat the oven to 325 degrees. Rinse the turkey with cool water and pat dry. In a sealable plastic bag, combine 2 tablespoons of the olive oil, 2 tablespoons of the Holiday Seasoning, lemons, orange, garlic and celery and shake to mix well. Stuff the turkey neck and main cavity with the lemon-garlic mixture. Don't bother sewing the cavities up. Leaving them open will add to the juices and flavor. Now use the remaining olive oil to coat the turkey breast and legs. Working with your hands to loosen the skin from the turkey breast, spread remaining Holiday Seasoning between the turkey skin and the turkey breast. Place the turkey on a rack in a roasting pan. Roast for 15 minutes per pound. Remove the turkey from the pan, place on the cutting surface and cover tightly with foil for 20 minutes before carving. Leave the lemon-garlic mixture in the turkey. This stuffing is to flavor the turkey not to eat. The keys to this juicy and flavorful turkey are the Holiday Seasoning blend and the additional flavor and cooking juices provided by the lemon-garlic "stuffing."

Note: See my Classic Holiday Gravy (page 149) and Holiday Stuffing recipes (pages 150 to 155).

Orange and Fennel Roasted Turkey with Victoria Taylor's Holiday Seasoning

PREPARATION TIME: 20 MINUTES / COOKING TIME: 3½ TO 5½ HOURS
SERVES: 6 TO 8

    1 family size turkey (15 to 22 pounds)
    3 tablespoons olive oil, divided
    4 to 5 tablespoons Victoria Taylor's Holiday Seasoning, divided
    1 lemon, cut into 1-inch pieces
    2 oranges, cut into 1-inch pieces
    1 cup fennel (mix of green and white portions), cut into 1-inch pieces
    2 carrots, cut into 1-inch pieces
    1 cup leafy celery tops, cut into 1-inch pieces

To prepare the turkey, remove the giblets and neck. Place the giblets and neck in 5 cups water and bring to a boil. Simmer for 1 hour, strain the stock and set it aside for the gravy and basting. Preheat the oven to 325 degrees. Rinse the turkey with cool water and pat dry. In a sealable plastic bag, combine 2 tablespoons of the olive oil, 2 tablespoons of the Holiday Seasoning, lemon, oranges, fennel, carrots and celery and shake to mix well. Stuff the turkey neck and main cavity with the orange-fennel mixture. Don't bother sewing the cavities up. Leaving them open will add to the juices and flavor. Now use the remaining olive oil to coat the turkey breast and legs. Working with your hands to loosen the skin from the turkey breast, spread remaining Holiday Seasoning between the turkey skin and the turkey breast and all over the turkey. Roast for 15 minutes per pound, basting occasionally with the turkey stock. Remove the turkey from the pan, place on a cutting surface and cover tightly with foil for 20 minutes before carving. Leave the orange-fennel mixture in the turkey. This stuffing is to flavor the turkey, not to eat. For stuffing ideas, see my Holiday Stuffing recipes on pages 150 through 155. The keys to this juicy and flavorful turkey are the Holiday Seasoning blend and the additional flavor and cooking juices provided by the orange-fennel "stuffing." The more traditional approach of stuffing the turkey with a

portion of the meal's bread-based stuffing just makes the stuffing wet and the turkey dry. That means dry turkey and less juices for gravy.

Note: This is the turkey recipe I have used at Thanksgiving for the last two years. The green leafy parts of the fennel add the most wonderful flavor to the roasted turkey.

Classic Holiday Gravy for the Turkey with Victoria Taylor's Holiday Seasoning

PREPARATION TIME: 10 MINUTES / COOKING TIME: 3 MINUTES
SERVES: GRAVY FOR 1 LARGE TURKEY AND LEFTOVERS

   1/4 cup flour
   1 teaspoon Victoria Taylor's Holiday Seasoning
   4 cups prepared turkey stock (Substitute 2 cups chicken
      stock with 2 cups water if necessary)
   1/4 cup dry sherry
   salt and pepper to taste

Once the roasted turkey has been removed from the roasting pan, pour all the juices from the pan into a tall container. The fat will settle on top. Return 3 tablespoons of the fat to the turkey pan. Discard the remaining fat, reserving the dark roasting juices. Place the pan over medium heat and whisk in the flour and Holiday Seasoning. Stir constantly until the fat and flour are mixed in clumps. Continuing to stir, slowly add the turkey stock 1/2 cup at a time until the gravy is fairly thin. Bring to a boil, adding more stock as needed. Add the sherry and the reserved dark pan juices. Simmer for 3 minutes. Add salt and pepper to taste.

Note: This recipe makes a rich dark gravy that is delicious with turkey, potatoes and stuffing. Gravy will continue to thicken on its own so keep it thinner before serving.

Apple, Corn Bread and Pecan Stuffing with Victoria Taylor's Holiday Seasoning

PREPARATION TIME: 45 MINUTES / COOKING TIME: 45 MINUTES
SERVES: 8 TO 10

1/2 cup (1 stick) butter, divided
1 1/2 cups chopped onion
2 tart apples, diced (MacIntosh or Granny Smith)
3/4 pound pork sausage
2 cups crumbled corn bread
2 cups crumbled white corn bread
2 cups crumbled whole wheat bread
3 tablespoons Victoria Taylor's Holiday Seasoning
sea salt to taste
1/3 cup fresh Italian parsley, chopped
1 cup pecan halves

Melt half the butter in a skillet. Add the onion and cook over low heat until lightly colored and tender, about 20 minutes. Transfer to a bowl. Melt the remaining butter and add the apples. Sauté slowly until lightly colored, but not too mushy, about 7 minutes. Add the apples to the bowl. Cook sausage in the skillet until brown and transfer to the bowl with a slotted spoon. Preheat the oven to 375 degrees. Add the corn bread, white corn bread, whole wheat bread, Holiday Seasoning, sea salt, Italian parsley and pecans to the sausage mixture in the bowl and toss gently. Transfer to a casserole and bake, uncovered, for 45 minutes. Baste stuffing with turkey or chicken stock, if desired.

Note: If fresh corn bread is not readily available, buy 2 corn muffins and use those for the 2 cups of crumbled corn bread.

Quick Apple Parmesan Stuffing with Victoria Taylor's Holiday Seasoning

PREPARATION TIME: 30 MINUTES / COOKING TIME: 45 MINUTES
SERVES: 6

    3 tablespoons butter
    2 medium onions, chopped
    2 tart unpeeled apples, cut into 3/4-inch pieces
    2 tablespoons Victoria Taylor's Holiday Seasoning
    3 cups crumbled white bread (French or Italian)
    1/2 cup fresh chopped Italian parsley
    1 cup grated Parmesan cheese

Preheat the oven to 375 degrees. Melt the butter in a skillet over medium-high heat. Sauté the onions and apples in the hot butter for 5 minutes. Stir in the Holiday Seasoning and remove from heat. In a large bowl, combine the onion mixture with the crumbled bread, fresh chopped Italian parsley and grated cheese. Transfer mixture to a casserole and bake, uncovered, for 45 minutes.

Note: Stuffing makes a great side dish anytime of the year. This quick stuffing recipe has no meat, so it's great with almost any main course.

Cornmeal Bacon Stuffing with Victoria Taylor's Holiday Seasoning

PREPARATION TIME: 45 MINUTES / COOKING TIME: 45 MINUTES
SERVES: 8

3 cups water
1 teaspoon salt
1 tablespoon butter
1 cup ground cornmeal
$^1/_2$ pound bacon
2 cups toasted white bread crumbs
2 celery stalks, cut into $^1/_2$-inch pieces
2 medium onions, diced
2 cloves garlic, minced
2 tablespoons Victoria Taylor's Holiday Seasoning
1 cup chicken stock

Use a large casserole (about 2 to 3 quarts) for this stuffing. Combine the water, salt and butter in a shallow saucepan and heat to a low boil. Add the cornmeal gradually, stirring constantly. Cook over low heat for 6 to 8 minutes or until the cornmeal has thickened, stirring constantly. Remove from heat. Spread the mixture (about $^1/_2$ inch thick) on a foil-covered baking sheet to cool. Cut the bacon into $^1/_2$-inch pieces with kitchen shears, then cook in a skillet until crisp. Drain the bacon on a paper towel, reserving 2 tablespoons of the drippings in the skillet. Use the food processor to make coarse crumbs with the white bread and toast under the broiler until light brown, watching closely to make sure they don't burn. Preheat the oven to 375 degrees. Heat the reserved 2 tablespoons of bacon drippings and sauté the celery, onions and garlic over low heat for 5 minutes. Add the bacon and Holiday Seasoning and cook for another 2 to 3 minutes. Remove from heat. Cut the cooled cornmeal into 1-inch squares and gently mix in a large bowl with chicken stock, toasted white bread crumbs and bacon mixture. Transfer to a casserole sprayed with nonstick cooking spray. Bake, uncovered, for 45 minutes.

Aromatic Vegetarian Stuffing with Victoria Taylor's Holiday Seasoning

PREPARATION TIME: 30 MINUTES / COOKING TIME: 1 HOUR
SERVES: 6 TO 8

2 tablespoons olive oil
2 cups (1/2-inch pieces) sweet potatoes
1 cup chopped onion
1 leek (white and light green portion only), finely chopped
1/2 cup pine nuts
2 cups (1/2-inch pieces) portobello mushrooms
1/4 cup marsala
3 tablespoons Victoria Taylor's Holiday Seasoning
3/4 cup chicken broth
1 1/2 cups whole wheat or multi-grain coarse bread crumbs

Heat the olive oil in a large skillet until hot but not smoking. Add the sweet potatoes, onion, leek and pine nuts. Sauté for 10 minutes. Add the mushrooms, marsala and Holiday Seasoning and cook for an additional 5 minutes. Transfer mixture to a large bowl to cool. Preheat the oven to 375 degrees. Add chicken broth and bread crumbs to vegetable mixture and toss gently. Transfer to a casserole and bake, uncovered, for 1 hour.

Note: Stuffing keeps well, refrigerated, as a leftover for 2 to 3 days. To reheat stuffing, add 1/2 cup chicken or turkey stock to the casserole to moisten and reheat at 325 degrees for 30 minutes.

Wild Rice and Mushroom Stuffing with Victoria Taylor's Holiday Seasoning

PREPARATION TIME: 30 MINUTES / COOKING TIME: 2 HOURS
SERVES: 8

> $1/2$ pound portobello mushrooms
> $1/2$ pound shiitake mushrooms
> 5 cups chicken broth
> 2 cups wild rice
> salt to taste
> 1 pound Italian sausage (sweet preferred to hot)
> 1 large carrot, peeled and cut into $1/2$-inch pieces
> 2 medium white onions, finely chopped
> 1 large unpeeled tart apple (Granny Smith or MacIntosh),
>   cut into $1/2$-inch pieces
> 2 tablespoons Victoria Taylor's Holiday Seasoning

Remove the stems from the mushrooms and finely chop. Chop the mushroom caps into $1/2$-inch pieces and set aside. Combine the chicken broth and mushroom stems in a pan and bring to a boil. Remove from heat and keep covered for 15 minutes. Add the wild rice and salt and bring to a boil. Simmer, covered, over low heat for 1 hour or until rice is tender, stirring occasionally and adding additional water or stock as needed. In a large skillet, crumble and brown the sausage. Transfer the cooked sausage to a plate with a slotted spoon, reserving the drippings in the skillet. Add the carrot, onions and reserved chopped mushroom caps to the skillet and sauté over medium heat for about 10 minutes. Add the apple and Holiday Seasoning to the skillet and cook for an additional 5 minutes. Preheat the oven to 375 degrees. Combine the sausage, rice and mushroom mixture in a bowl and mix well. Transfer to a large casserole and bake, uncovered, for 1 hour.

Note: Portobello mushrooms start out as baby-bellas, which are also called cremini mushrooms. The smaller baby-bellas are a bit milder in flavor compared to the large full-grown portobellos.

Sausage Stuffing with Cranberries and Apricots with Victoria Taylor's Holiday Seasoning

PREPARATION TIME: 30 MINUTES / COOKING TIME: 1 HOUR
SERVES: 6 TO 8

2 tablespoons olive oil
2 medium onions, chopped
3 cloves garlic, minced
3/4 pound sausage (sweet preferred to spicy)
3/4 cup dried apricots, coarsely chopped
3/4 cup chopped fresh Italian parsley
1/2 cup dried cranberries
grated zest of 1 organic (if possible) orange
juice from 1 orange
2 tablespoons Victoria Taylor's Holiday Seasoning
1/2 teaspoon salt
3 cups torn white bread
1 (14 1/2-ounce) can chicken broth

Heat the olive oil in a large skillet until hot but not smoking. Add the onions and garlic and cook until translucent, about 10 minutes. Add the sausage and cook until brown. Preheat the oven to 375 degrees. Transfer the sausage mixture to a large bowl. Add the apricots, parsley, cranberries, orange zest, orange juice, Holiday Seasoning and salt to the sausage mixture and mix well. Stir in the torn bread pieces and chicken broth. Transfer to a casserole and bake, uncovered, for 1 hour.

Note: Use an organic orange if possible for this recipe. The non-organic ones may have a very bitter flavor in their skins, which makes the orange zest taste harsh. This dish makes a colorful presentation in a casserole dish because of the dark red cranberries and the orange apricots.

Spiced Chunky Applesauce with Victoria Taylor's Mulling Spices

PREPARATION TIME: 10 MINUTES / COOKING TIME: 20 MINUTES
SERVES: 8

   4 MacIntosh apples, peeled and cut into 1-inch pieces
   4 Granny Smith apples, peeled and cut into 1-inch pieces
   2 cups water
   juice of 1 lemon
   1 cup sugar
   2 tablespoons Victoria Taylor's Mulling Spices, wrapped and tied in
      cheesecloth

Combine the apples, water, lemon juice and sugar in a deep microwave-safe casserole. Add the bundle of Mulling Spices to the dish. Microwave for 10 minutes in the microwave at full power. Stir well, pressing the apples into the liquid. Microwave for another 10 minutes. Use a slotted spoon or a potato masher to mash the mixture until coarsely mixed. Cool the applesauce at room temperature. Before refrigerating, remove the bundle of Mulling Spices and stir the applesauce and cover.

Note: The freshness of this applesauce recipe comes in part from the microwave process, which avoids a long boiling time. Serve it cold from the refrigerator, or heat it up as a dessert and serve with a spoonful of vanilla ice cream.

Spiced Pears with Victoria Taylor's Mulling Spices

PREPARATION TIME: 10 MINUTES / COOKING TIME: 30 TO 40 MINUTES
SERVES: 4

    4 fresh pears (1 per person), sliced in half lengthwise and cored
        (Bartlett or Anjou pears work well but red pears are nice also)
    4 cups apple cider or apple juice
    1/4 cup Victoria Taylor's Mulling Spices

Preheat the oven to 350 degrees. Place pears cut side down in a glass baking dish just large enough to hold them. Pour apple cider or apple juice over the pears until they are almost covered. Sprinkle with Mulling Spices (1 tablespoon per whole pear). Cover with foil. Bake for 30 to 40 minutes or until pears are tender but not too soft.

Note: This can be a first course served with a slice of Cheddar cheese or a delicious dessert served with whipped cream or ice cream.

Old-Fashioned Apple Pie with Victoria Taylor's Pie Spices

PREPARATION TIME: 30 MINUTES / COOKING TIME: 1½ HOURS
SERVES: 8

The Crust:
    2½ cups flour
    1 tablespoon sugar
    ¾ teaspoon salt
    1 cup (2 sticks) chilled unsalted butter, cut into ½-inch pieces
    6 tablespoons (or more) ice water

The Filling:
    ½ cup sugar
    ¼ cup packed light brown sugar
    2 tablespoons flour
    2 tablespoons Victoria Taylor's Pie Spices
    3 pounds hard apples, peeled, cored and thinly sliced
    milk
    additional sugar and Victoria Taylor's Pie Spices

For the Crust: Blend the flour, sugar and salt in a food processor. Add the butter and pulse until mixture resembles coarse cornmeal. Add ice water and process until moist clumps form, adding more water by teaspoonfuls if dough is dry. Gather into a ball. Divide into 2 portions. Flatten each portion into a disk.

For the Filling: Combine the sugar, brown sugar, flour and Pie Spices in large bowl and mix well. Add the apples and toss to mix well.

Position oven rack in lowest third of oven. Preheat the oven to 400 degrees. Roll out 1 dough disk into a 12-inch circle on a floured surface. Transfer to a round 9-inch glass pie dish. Fold edge under, forming high-standing rim. Add the filling. Roll out second dough disk into a 13-inch circle on a floured surface. Place on top of the filling and gently press edges of top and bottom crust together; crimp. Brush top with milk. Sprinkle lightly with additional sugar and Pie Spices. Bake pie for 10 minutes. Reduce oven temperature to 375 degrees. Continue baking for 1 hour and 20 minutes or until juices bubble thickly and crust is deep golden, covering edges with foil if browning too quickly. Cool on a wire rack for 1 hour before serving.

Note: Serve with vanilla ice cream or slightly sweetened whipped cream.

Apple Crisp with Victoria Taylor's Pie Spices

PREPARATION TIME: 10 MINUTES / COOKING TIME: 45 TO 60 MINUTES
SERVES: 8

Apple Mixture:
8 MacIntosh or Cortland apples, peeled and sliced
¼ cup sugar
½ cup chopped walnuts
2 teaspoons Victoria Taylor's Pie Spices

Topping:
1 cup rolled oats
⅓ cup flour
½ cup (1 stick) butter, softened
½ cup packed brown sugar
½ teaspoon salt

For the Apple Mixture: Combine the apples, sugar and walnuts in a bowl and mix well. Sprinkle generously with the Pie Spices. Place in a large, shallow glass baking dish, such as an 8x12-inch Pyrex dish.

For the Topping: Preheat the oven to 350 degrees. Combine the oatmeal, flour, butter, brown sugar and salt in a bowl and mix well. Sprinkle on top of the apples. Bake for 45 to 60 minutes or until topping is crisp. Serve with whipped cream or vanilla ice cream.

Note: When serving with whipped cream, sprinkle a dusting of Pie Spices on the whipped cream for the finishing touch.

Pumpkin Pie with Victoria Taylor's Pie Spices

PREPARATION TIME: 30 MINUTES
REFRIGERATION TIME: 1¹/₂ HOURS / COOKING TIME: 1 HOUR
SERVES: 8

The Crust:
    1¹/₄ cups flour
    ¹/₂ cup (1 stick) cold unsalted butter
    ¹/₂ teaspoon salt
    2 to 4 tablespoons ice water

The Filling:
    1 (15-ounce) can solid-pack pumpkin (about 2 cups)
    1 cup heavy cream
    ¹/₂ cup whole milk
    2 large eggs
    ¹/₂ cup packed light brown sugar
    1 tablespoon Victoria Taylor's Pie Spices
    ¹/₄ teaspoon salt

For the Crust: Blend the flour, butter and salt in a food processor and pulse until mixture resembles coarse cornmeal. Add 2 tablespoons ice water and process until moist clumps form, adding more water by teaspoonfuls if dough is dry. Gather into a ball. Flatten into a disk. Refrigerate for at least 1 hour prior to rolling. Roll out dough into a 14-inch round on a lightly floured surface and fit into a 9-inch glass pie plate. Crimp edge and prick bottom all over. Chill 30 minutes. Position rack in middle of oven. Preheat the oven to 375 degrees. Using a fork make holes in the crust before baking. Bake in the middle of the oven for 20 to 25 minutes or until lightly golden. Cool on a wire rack.

For the Filling: Whisk filling ingredients in a bowl. Pour into the prepared pie shell. Bake pie in the middle of the oven for 45 to 50 minutes or until filling is set but center still trembles slightly. (Filling will continue to set as pie cools). Transfer to a wire rack to cool completely. Serve topped with whipped cream and sprinkled with a dusting of Pie Spices.

Chocolate-Covered Strawberries with Perfumed Whipped Cream with Victoria Taylor's Pie Spices

PREPARATION TIME: 15 MINUTES
SERVES: 4

The Strawberries:
    12 ounces best quality bittersweet chocolate
    1 1/2 tablespoons solid white vegetable shortening
    fancy wooden picks
    25 to 30 large strawberries

The Whipped Cream:
    1 cup heavy cream
    1 tablespoon confectioners' sugar
    1 teaspoon vanilla extract
    1 teaspoon Victoria Taylor's Pie Spices

For the Strawberries: Use a double boiler to melt the chocolate and the shortening until creamy. Remove from heat and let cool for about 5 minutes. Using the wooden picks, dip each strawberry in the chocolate until half covered and transfer to a waxed paper-lined baking sheet. Place immediately in the refrigerator to let the chocolate set.

For the Whipped Cream: Beat the cream in a bowl until peaks form then add the confectioners' sugar, vanilla and Pie Spices. Continue to beat until stiff. Serve the strawberries with a bowl of the perfumed whipped cream for dipping.

Hot Mulled Cranberry Juice with Oranges with Victoria Taylor's Mulling Spices

PREPARATION TIME: 5 MINUTES / COOKING TIME: 20 MINUTES
SERVES: 8

    1 (64-ounce) bottle cranberry juice
    1 orange, sliced
    3 tablespoons Victoria Taylor's Mulling Spices

Pour the cranberry juice into a medium saucepan. Add the orange slices. Use a small piece of cheesecloth to tie up the Mulling Spices. Add to the cranberry juice and simmer for 20 minutes. Serve warm in mugs.

Note: Add 1/4 cup of vodka or light rum to the mulled cranberry juice for a holiday cocktail alternative.

Mulled Cider with Victoria Taylor's Mulling Spices

PREPARATION TIME: 5 MINUTES / COOKING TIME: 20 MINUTES
SERVES: 8

    1/4 cup Victoria Taylor's Mulling Spices
    1/2 gallon apple cider

Tie the Mulling Spices in a small piece of cheesecloth with kitchen string. Simmer the bundle of mulling spices in the apple cider in a saucepan for 15 to 20 minutes. Serve in warm mugs.

Note: My Mulling Spices include whole anise stars that have a hint of licorice flavor. I love that flavor note because it balances the sweetness of the cloves and cinnamon.

Index